BIGGIE

VOLETTA WALLACE REMEMBERS HER SON

BIGGIE

with Tremell McKenzie

POETRY BY VOLETTA WALLACE

ATRIA BOOKS
New York London Toronto Sydney

ATRIA BOOKS

1230 Avenue of the Americas
New York, NY 10020

ISBN-13: 978-0-7434-7020-9
ISBN-10:   0-7434-7020-6

First Atria Books hardcover edition October 2005

10 9 8 7 6 5 4 3 2 1

ATRIA BOOKS is a trademark of Simon & Schuster, Inc.

Manufactured in the United States of America

For information regarding special discounts for bulk purchases,
please contact Simon & Schuster Special Sales at 1-800-456-6798
or business@simonandschuster.com.

DEDICATION

a heartfelt dedication to my son and grandkids

Dedicated to my late son Christopher Wallace

and to my two grandchildren T'yanna Dream

and Christopher Jordan

CONTENTS

FOREWORD

blessed spirits such as his are few & far between

I'm honored and pleased to write this foreword, not only because Ms. Voletta Wallace is my dear friend but more so because her book offers a unique contribution to literature, as her perspective on her son is so real and intimate.

Biggie needs no introduction. Readers know him through his recorded lyrical offerings. There are not many scholars or preachers—living or passed—who touch such a responsive chord as the late great Christopher Wallace, among youth and adults alike. Blessed spirits such as his are few and far between.

This book offers a glimpse into the life of the man behind the lyrics. The content has been carefully selected and the results make fascinating reading. There is a continuity of thought that compels the reader to begin and finish the book in one sitting.

Reading this extremely well-written and well-documented memoir caused me to reminisce about my own experience with B.I.G. This is a mother's perspective on her beloved son's life, representing only a fraction of the whole that was Christopher's rich and dramatic life.

Ms. Wallace gives me and all of us added insight into the man we were privileged to know and love—me as his former wife and still mother of his child, you as his friends and fans. Her work is deeply inspiring and reveals faith and genuine pride in B.I.G., and also reinforces his importance in hip-hop culture.

I want to express my gratitude to her and the continuing outpouring of love and support that inspired this publication.

Yours truly,

Faith

the man
we were
privileged
to **know**
and LOVE

is there
life
after
death?

VOLETTA WALLACE REMEMBERS HER SON

BIGGIE

COMING TO
AMERICA

Is there life after death?

Panic and fear had made time stand still for me. I could no longer hear nor comprehend anything going on around me. All the sounds that I could still hear were coming from inside my own body. I could hear every breath that I took, and then I became aware of my heartbeat and it grew louder and louder in my ears, making it impossible to answer all the questions in my head. Is there life after death? Could I have done more with my life? Are all my affairs in order? What do I have to leave behind to the one I love? And, will he be okay?

They say when you are faced with death, your life flashes before your eyes. I know for me that statement held true. My entire life flashed before eyes, and it started from the very beginning.

OUR WORLD

Our world, encroached with faults and hate, ideas and thoughts, Shortcomings and regrets.

Our world, caressed with fears and mistakes, continued taste on rainfall and tears;

Our world, a creation of admiration and desire,

Of luster and dreams, smiles and hopes, youths and friendships.

Our world, bridged with deaths, disheartened looks, unselfish passion, Short hellos and long good-byes;

Our world, a frozen fountain Of wanting; wanting to know, to live, to love, to touch, To cherish, to grow, to give, to accept.

To grasp and reflect. To remember, that in our world: A life lost, is a life missed. A life gained, is a life blessed.

A life youthful Is a life Beautiful...

I was transported back to Trelawny, Jamaica, and the first house that I can remember living in. It was just one huge room. The room had a table, a bed, and three little chairs. Thinking back on it, the house was not really a house where one could live and enjoy. It was just a place to sleep that provided shelter when the weather was bad. Most of our living took place outside the house and in the yard.

live and enjoy

My family was close-knit. My mother believed in and enforced family. She wouldn't tolerate any fighting between my brother, Valen, my sister, Ruby, and me. If she caught a whiff of us fighting, everyone could expect a beating. My grandmother lived nearby in a house that was exactly the same as ours on the inside. The only difference was on the outside, where my grandmother had a big thatched roof made from coconut palm leaves. My older siblings stayed with my grandmother at night because there just wasn't enough room for everyone in our little one-room house; during the day they would be at school.

As the youngest, I often felt like an only child.

My father worked hard as a butcher and a farmer, while my mother stayed at home to take care of us. By the time I was seven years old, my father had saved enough money to buy land and build us a bigger house on a farm with a lot of land. I somehow knew even at age seven that we had been poor and that the farm was a step up for my family. It provided us with everything we needed.

I wish I could say that I had a great relationship with my older siblings, especially my sister, Ruby—but I can't. We were worlds apart. Even when I was old enough to interact with my brother and sister regularly, I didn't really want to. I preferred the company of my mother and father instead, and that hasn't changed.

To say there was sibling rivalry between Ruby and me would be an understatement. All of them teased me, calling me "Mama's girl" and "Daddy's girl." But I caught the most grief from my sister, Ruby. In fact, she was responsible for the first ass-whipping that I got from my dad.

From time to time Ruby would have to watch me when my mother was working. My stomach would drop when I knew that my mother would be leaving me alone with Ruby. It would be torture for me. I never knew what kind of mood Ruby would be in—not that it was ever a good mood. But sometimes she would hit me for no reason. If she was bored, she would find a reason to yell and scream at me. I was growing real tired of the routine: Boss Voletta around. Hit Voletta. Yell at Voletta. This would go on day in and day out, but I never said anything to my parents. I don't know why. Maybe because she was the oldest and we were raised to respect our elders.

One day when my mother had to go to town and left me with Ruby, she started her usual with me. Then she hauled off and knocked the hell out of me. That was the last straw. While I was much smaller and couldn't beat her physically, I had quite a mouth on me and I finally yelled back, "You stupid bitch!"

Everything went quiet. We both just kind of stared at each other, listening as if what I'd said had come from someone or someplace else. My eyes were wide and my fists were balled and all was quiet except for my own heavy breathing.

Had I won this battle with Ruby? Would she leave me alone from now on? She seemed to be in shock but she wasn't. In fact, she was elated. I didn't realize it yet, but I had made her day. I had sealed the deal and guaranteed myself a serious ass-whipping and she knew it.

She told me, "As soon as Mommy gets home, I'm telling! And you know what? I can't wait!" In my mind Ruby was pure evil. I wanted to scream, I wanted to hurt her, but she had won.

She was so excited about telling on me that her excitement alone had me scared and made my stomach nervous. I didn't really realize what I had called her. Of course, *bitch* means a female dog. But in Jamaica dogs are not treated like pets—they are the lowest things on the island. It was just a word that I'd heard since I was little, and for me the word was an experiment. I felt good calling her a bitch, but clearly I had not thought of the consequences of using the word.

My friend Gayle and me.

When my mother came home, Ruby greeted her halfway into the yard.

"You will not believe what your little princess called me," she said with glee. "She called me a *bitch!*"

Ruby never said what had led up to the name-calling, but at that point it didn't matter. My mother waited patiently for my father to come home. When my father got home, my mother said to my sister, "Ruby, tell Charlie what his daughter did." I didn't wait for her to tell him. I left the house and hid out back. I watched him leave the house to go down to a tree and search the branches for a switch to beat me with. I couldn't even keep looking because I knew what this was leading to.

Then he called for me. I knew I was going to get something when I heard him calling. The next thing I felt and heard was loud swooshes as he caught me right on the leg, and I didn't wait to get another one. I ran and screamed so loud that all the neighbors heard and were looking to see what had happened. My legs were completely numb, but I didn't stop running. I ran straight to my grandmother's house. I don't know how I got there. I don't remember seeing anyone or anything. This happened on a Saturday, and the next morning my grandmother told me that I had to go home. But I wouldn't leave.

She went to church and I followed right behind her in the same dirty little dress that I had had on since my Saturday whipping. After church, she walked me back to my house and told my father that Ruby had been hitting me and that she had provoked the name-calling and deserved to be called whatever she was called. My grandmother told my father not to hit me again. I'm not sure what else she said and I'll never know, but my father never hit me again.

The fights continued between Ruby and me because she continued her bossy nastiness and I continued to retaliate verbally. I don't remember exactly what happened to cause our next big argument, but I called her a "bastard." Needless to say, my mother slapped me so hard I saw stars. The comment had insulted my mother, something I had no intention of doing. She later said to me that she didn't have any illegitimate children and that my sister and I were not cats and dogs so we needed to stop behaving like animals. I decided not to speak to my sister again for a long time. I thought it was best, because if I did, she would eventually have made me say something to her for which I would have gotten killed. So I kept my distance from her until she left home.

She eventually found herself a lover, had a baby, and moved away. Sad to say, Ruby and I never bonded the way we should have. I grew close to all of my other siblings, except for her. Deep down I wish we did have a kiss-and-hug, share-clothes type of relationship the way sisters should have, but we never did. She went her way and I went mine. We never got to really know each other. We were perfect strangers in the same household.

Outside of the tumultuous relationship with my sister, my life in Jamaica was peaceful and filled with long, beautiful days going into the fields with my father. He would always go with a donkey or on his bicy-

beautiful days

cle. I was the one he would take with him to the fields, not to work but for company. I was his little talking pet that he would always carry with him. When we got there, I would sit under a tree watching him work. I would be playing and daydreaming all by myself. When it was time for him to take a break, I would get his lunch ready and we would sit together and eat under a tree until it was time for him to go back to work or for us to go home. If my father didn't get home in time to eat with everyone else, he would call me to come sit with him and we would share dinner, too. No matter what he was eating or how much he had, he would always offer me some. He didn't do that with anyone else. I guess—no, I know for a fact—that Ruby was right about one thing . . . I was "Daddy's little girl."

■ ■ ■

My long days with my father ended way too soon for me, but it was time for me to start school. The Jamaican school system was, and still is, very different from that of the United States. In Jamaica you go to nursery school, then kindergarten, and finally to grade school, which ends at the sixth grade. After the sixth grade, education was no longer free, so at fifteen years old if you had not received a scholarship to continue your education and your parents could not afford to pay high school tuition—which was expensive and did not include your books—your education ended.

The other option was to travel far away to a community or public school in Kingston, Jamaica. But because of the limited modes of

transportation, community school was not an option for the majority. I, however, had family that lived in the suburbs of Kingston, which was mostly farmland, so I felt right at home and was able to continue my education.

So, when I was sixteen years old, I packed up and went to live with a distant "aunt." Technically, she was not my biological aunt but the aunt of one of my cousins. She was wonderful to allow me to stay with her while I went to school. And I was pleased to help her out around her house and with chores, especially during her pregnancy, when she really needed the help. We were a godsend to each other. Her husband wasn't around much because he worked hard.

I also had a busy schedule. I would go into the city to attend school and I worked part-time at a travel agency. My job was the first place I got a glimpse that there was a world outside of Jamaica. There were so many brochures and magazines about traveling the world, and I would spend hours just daydreaming about my fancy life outside Jamaica. One country in particular stuck out for me—the United States. And little did I know that my exodus to America might come quicker than planned.

On the night that my aunt went into labor, I had already gone to bed and she had a friend take her to the hospital. I had to stay behind to watch her small son, who slept in the room with me. Her husband was still at work.

At one point that night, the door to the room opened and someone came in. It was my aunt's husband, who I thought had gone to the hospital to be with his wife after he'd finished his shift.

I am a pretty hard sleeper so I didn't notice that he was in my room until I felt this presence hovering over my bed. I opened my eyes to find his face hovering over my face and his hands touching my body. When I realized it was him and what was happening, I swung violently at his face—intending to take his eyes out. I slapped his face and screamed at the top of my lungs. Even in the dark, I could see his eyes widen at the thought of me telling his wife and the humiliation he would face.

He glanced over at his son, who was in a bed on the opposite side of the room, then looked at me and started to back out of the room, apologizing. He said in hushed tones that he was sorry and that he had never done anything like this before. He said he didn't know or realize what he was doing.

When he left the room, I was scared and angry. I knew that I was no longer at a home away from home and that I had to leave. He had never done anything to me in the days leading up to that night to make me think he was capable of doing something like that. In fact, I didn't think he even noticed me. I stayed awake that night crying about all the things that would suddenly come to an end, such as school and my part-time job. But my instincts told me to go and not look back.

When I woke up the next day, I wrote a letter to my brother, Valen, telling him that he should send a telegram to me right away, and that the telegram should say a relative was sick and my assistance was needed back home immediately. He wrote me back wanting to know what was going on and why I was doing this. He wanted details immediately. I told him that I would let him know everything as soon as he sent the telegram and got me out of Kingston without upsetting my aunt and her new baby.

Valen sent the telegram soon after and my aunt understood. When I got home, I told Valen everything, and he wanted to go and kick her husband's ass. I told him that he had not harmed me physically and that I was able to go on with my life and that I felt no reason to upset my aunt's home when I could just leave. I never told my mother or anyone else.

This thing took me completely by surprise. My mother had never sat me down and given me one of those talks about men. She was old-fashioned and trusted the world. I'm not sure how it would have affected her if I'd told her. I just figured it would have done more harm than good.

Despite not being able to finish high school, I made up my mind that I would work hard and make a good life for myself. I'd watched my father work hard and save enough money to buy land and build us a

freedom

house with his own hands. So I knew firsthand that through hard work I could do it, too.

■ ■ ■

I found myself once again back home in Trelawny, but this time I could not just settle in. They say the grass is always greener on the other side—and for me the other side was America. I was fascinated with going to America. I continued to read anything about the States that I could get my hands on.

The thought of England crossed my mind a few times, but the people, to me, came across as snobs. Despite having family in London, I had no desire to go there because it seemed like such a bore. It made me think of people with umbrellas and damp, old streets. London was gray and dull. But the United States of America had color and style. I knew that I would one day go there.

I needed to experience all of these things firsthand, especially the snow, because it seemed to make everything more bright and beautiful. At least that's how it looked in the pictures in the magazines and brochures that the

This is my brother and mother.

travel agency received each month. There were a lot of pictures of New York, which only served to fuel my imagination and dreams of living the way the people in America lived. I was in love with the United States. Everyone there seemed so rich. Everyone lived in a big house. And even if they didn't live in a big house, they lived in tall luxury apartment buildings with fireplaces. Oh, and the cars. All of them were big and sleek and new. The clothes would be only the finest and most fashionable. I could occupy myself for hours just daydreaming about what my fancy life in the United States was going to be like.

While my daydreams were nice and allowed my long, hot days to go by faster, I was still a realist. How was I going to get to America? I was never a person who believed in luck. I believed that I would create my own destiny through education and hard work. I was raised to believe that you achieve the things you want through hard work, and this was drilled into my head with words and by example. There was no way

...new york

around it. More important, I was taught that nothing is just handed to you, nothing is free . . . nothing. You must work for all that you get.

But on this day, things would be different. Out of the blue it appeared in the mail. It was from Jules Georgeson, House of Fashion. My old boss from the employment agency told me that it was an invitation.

"Do you know, you can use this and travel to the United States because you have a way with fashion. They would look at you and you would have no problem," he said.

I could not believe it. And I didn't know what to say or what to do next. When would I leave? What would I pack? What would I do when I got there? This invitation to New York was to change my world. I hadn't entered a contest or anything like that. I was just chosen. Here I was, actually going to a place that I had already visited a million times in my head.

I didn't think about being a young lady alone in a strange country. As a matter of fact, I didn't have any of the fears or anxieties that a person of any age, let alone a nineteen-year-old girl, might have about leaving her small island home for the first time and going to another country and being all by herself.

My family had friends in New York whom we contacted, and I was planning to stay with a friend of the family's so that I would not be all alone. But I was too excited to think about that. I was so naive that I didn't consider anything except the adventure.

■ ■ ■

...leaving

It was 1969 and I was sitting on a Pan Am airplane with my heart doing back-flips. It was my first trip to America. Hell, it was my first trip to any place on an airplane. It was a three-and-a-half-hour jouney to the United States. I was tremendously nervous and excited at the same time. I couldn't even eat the tuna fish sandwiches they served on the plane. I was going to America. I was headed to the lap of luxury and leaving my simple life far behind me. Though I remember what kind of food I was served on my first plane trip, the rest is simply a blur. I had dreamed so much about what it would be like being on a plane to America that most of that ride felt more like déjà vu.

I spent the entire plane ride daydreaming and wondering, tears flowing down my face, what the hell was in store for me once the plane landed. I had envisioned a place of wealth and glamour, of freedom and opportunity. That's what the photos in *Life* and *Ebony* magazines showed me. That's what I saw on the television programs that I used to watch—wealth and glamour.

my simple life

And I was going to the "Big Apple" no less—home to the Empire State Building and skyscrapers. This was the home of the rich and glamorous, and I was going there to be one of them. I imagined having a maid and a driver, furs and fancy clothes. Of course, I was going to have a husband, a nice big home, and beautiful children. That was my dream—my American dream.

I arrived at New York's John F. Kennedy Airport with my eyes wide shut and ready to take in everything. As the plane was landing, I could see from my window this grand city of lights—lights that I had never seen before. It was exceptionally beautiful. When I got off the airplane, I was amazed just by the number of people. Every inch of space in the airport seemed to be filled with them, and they were all moving so fast. I made my way to customs, then baggage claim, got my bags, and went to the ground transportation section, where I was instructed to catch a taxicab to the Bronx, where I would be staying with friends of my family's.

There, my rose-colored glasses were smacked off my face. On my way out of Brooklyn toward the Bronx, a cabdriver was standing across from a police officer, yelling at the top of his lungs, "You motherfucker, you better get out of my face, motherfucker!" I quickly got into a cab, afraid, thinking, *Is this what freedom of speech really means?*

Those were the first words I heard come out of an American's mouth. This scene was so harsh and scary and looked as if it was going to get scarier as the police officer approached the cabbie. I was alarmed

jolt of reality

because this cabdriver wasn't using this language with just anyone. He was cursing at a *police officer.* I thought to myself, *What kind of place is this!* This was a side of America I had never considered. I was faced with a new reality that brought with it fear and anxiety. I started to feel lost and alone in this strange country. If this had happened in Jamaica, jail would have been the cabdriver's home for the night, because this sort of freedom of speech did not exist there.

I got my final jolt of reality when the cab pulled up in front of a tenement building on a narrow, one-way street, 111 Tudor Place, in the Bronx off the Grand Concourse. Was this to be my new home? And the picture became clear—this part of America was nothing like what I'd grown up seeing in *Ebony.* All I could say was "This is it?"

I was disappointed, but still hopeful. I knew there had to be more in this big country. I just needed time, money, and a plan. I came up with a five-year plan to work hard and save all my money. And by the end of the five years if I didn't want to stay in America, I would take the money I had saved

and build a house on some of my parents' land in Trelawny.

The first thing I needed to put my plan into action was a job. After a couple of weeks, I landed a job working for a psychiatrist, at $18 a day. Then I found a furnished room to rent for $14 a week. This dingy, cold little basement room had a tiny twin bed in the corner. I shared the kitchen with the owner and another man who was also renting a room. I also had to share the bathroom with them. I stayed there for six months. My next place was a step up into a small studio on St. Francis Place off Franklin Avenue in Brooklyn. The rent almost tripled to $35 a week, but I also took babysitting jobs to supplement my income.

I was blessed with a strong sense of pride because even while living in that little basement-hole studio apartment, I felt that I had a lot more than many others out there. I knew there were nicer apartments but this was *my* apartment. I wasn't living off anybody. I lived in a $35-a-week studio and I knew this wasn't the last step for me. I had a plan. I was striving and preparing to make a future for myself.

sense of pride

Although I was working hard, I needed to work smarter to improve my financial situation. My new goal was to get my GED. I enrolled in a night school and focused on improving myself. It never occurred to me that I had adapted to this country and had been navigating the system all by myself. America had grown on me and I didn't even realize how much. I naturally grabbed on to all of the things that were good about the country and stayed far away from the filth. I went to work, I went to school, I went home, I babysat. That was my routine five days a week, sometimes six. I had created a safe little world of my own—my cocoon, so to speak. I said my prayers every day and followed the Christian ethics I'd brought with me from Jamaica. I never begged. I borrowed money a few times but I paid it back as soon as I could. I was making an honest living for myself. Hell, America had grown on me.

Two years into my plan, I decided to stay in America. I decided that I would create the American dream I had dreamt so many years ago. I somehow felt it was all possible. I would settle down, have the house, the clothes, and the family. I would apply to become a citizen. This was going to be my permanent home.

american dream

ONE LIE AND
A BABY

Deep
breath.
One more
thing
I didn't
see
coming.

I just had a complete physical three months ago and I was given a clean bill of health. So why do I feel lumps in my breast? They feel like stones and one of the lumps is hurting like hell. [Deep breath.] Just one more thing I didn't see coming.

You never know when life is going to send you a curveball. Despite all my efforts to stay on top of everything in my life—such as going to the dentist every six months like clockwork, getting my yearly physical, and just making an effort to stay ahead of this game [life]—the unimaginable always seemed to creep into my world and give it a real shake. Something always seemed to happen to let me know that I wasn't in control at all.

I was about twenty-three years old the last time I thought I had all my bases covered and was in complete control of my life. . . .

I had put myself on course to be a success and would let nothing distract me. I was working, going to school, and saving my money. I was running my life like a well-oiled machine—looking to stay one step ahead of anyone or anything that might get in my way. So I thought.

I had been in New York two years and was working on my plans with a one-track mind. My best friend, Laurice, who was also from Jamaica, had been in the United States for more than seven years. Opposites really do attract. Laurice was a real social butterfly. I was more of a homebody who preferred to stay on the sidelines at social events. Laurice thrived in the company of others and looked for any reason at all to have a party.

We were on the phone with each other constantly. I mean, if we weren't out shopping together, we were on the phone with each other. We talked about everything. I mostly talked about my life after finishing school and how I was going to make a lot of money. Our conversations usually rounded out with her telling me that I spent entirely too much time working and going to school, and then inviting me to her next party.

It was a Saturday evening and Laurice was having one of her get-togethers. I was too tired to make it, but she called me on the phone to make sure to keep me abreast of all that was going on at the party. She called like a sportscaster, giving me a complete play-by-play of all that was happening. While we were talking on the phone, I heard someone in the background ask her, "Who is this in the picture?"

Me, my son's father, and Gayle.

and Laurice yelled back, "Oh, that's my best friend, Voletta. As a matter of fact, I'm on the phone with her now."

His name was Selwyn and he had noticed my picture among all of the other pictures of family and friends that Laurice had on her mantel. He said that he wanted to meet me, and from that day on he set his sights on me.

I decided to go to one of Laurice's parties, with a little encouragement from her. It was an opportunity for me to break out of my routine. I noticed him from the very beginning because of his height. He walked with a look of confidence and authority.

opposites attract

I later found out that look of authority came from Selwyn's being twenty years older than me. I didn't notice the age difference at first. He never seemed like an "old" person to me. In fact, I felt comfortable around Selwyn from the beginning. He reminded me of a big brother—or even a father figure—that I so desperately missed.

He would call me to ask if I had eaten or to ask, "Did you cover your head in the rain today?" He would even ask if I was getting enough rest. This concern for me opened the doors to trust. Our conversations were always about me, and there was never any sexual talk. He treated me with the utmost respect. I found myself "in like" with having a fatherly figure back in my life. It felt wonderful having someone around who had such a genuine concern for my well-being. He made me feel like a little girl again—like his little girl—and it felt wonderful.

For two years I had been working, going to school, hanging out with Laurice, and attending some of her many house gatherings to break the monotony in my life, and that was it, that was the extent of my life. Selwyn brought a little spice into it.

When I met him, I wasn't looking for him to be my savior. In my mind, if he was even going to be a part of my life, he would have to wait. I knew that I would eventually marry and have a family of my own. I even knew that I wanted three children and a big house. But that wouldn't be for a while. I had things I needed to do first. I had been working so hard and I didn't want to stop short. I was realistic enough to know that no one was just going to hand me my dreams, I had to work for them.

Although I think most women back then, and even now, look outside themselves and expect a man to supply them with the big house and make their dreams come true, I had a different idea. Deep down inside, I felt solely responsible for making all of my dreams come true. I felt that even if I were married, I needed to be prepared to contribute if I wanted to make all my dreams come true.

I was so busy preparing for this great life in the future that I wasn't living my life in the present. But Selwyn gave me a new perspective. He would take me to the park and we would hold hands and talk. He would take me to nice restaurants to eat. We would go to the movies. In fact, the first movie I ever saw was with Selwyn. It was *Shaft,* directed by Gordon Parks and starring Richard Roundtree. It was about a black man who brought justice everywhere he went. He was like a superhero. I enjoyed it.

I was exposed to so many different things through Selwyn—so many new tastes, new sights. In two months with him, I got to see more of New York than I had in my two years of living there. Before I met Selwyn, I have to admit, my life was just a boring routine and I had programmed myself to just go through the motions. I could certainly see spending the rest of my life with the person who had introduced me to this big, exciting world that existed outside the walls of my small apartment. For the first time I was looking forward to things that weren't just part of my five-year plan. Suddenly, I was looking forward to Friday. He brought spontaneity into my life and it felt good. What was I doing before? I had no idea that I needed some excitement in my life until he came along.

Somewhere in the midst of this whirlwind of excitement, I got sick. I was still working and going to school and taking care of myself, but I got sick and couldn't seem to shake it. I had weighed less than a hundred pounds when I'd first come to the United States—ninety-eight to be exact—but it seemed as though I had lost ten pounds in just a couple of weeks. I decided I should go to the doctor because it was becoming impossible to keep up with work and school feeling the way I was feeling.

After examining me, the doctor told me that I was pregnant. *Pregnant!* He had to be kidding. That was not in my plans, not at all. My mind was racing. I was not ready to have a baby. Aside from the shock of the baby, I think I was more upset that my plans for the future would be altered or possibly ruined. I considered myself too immature to be a mother, but it wasn't going to stop this baby from coming. My mind was racing and going back to the plans I'd made for my life. Where was my big, beautiful house, my husband, and my profession? *Damn, I'm screwed!*

Having an abortion never even entered my mind, and looking back, it would have been the easiest thing for me to do. Somehow I managed to go into complete denial of the pregnancy. My naive little mind figured that I could pray the baby away, and I tried. I prayed every single day and every minute that I thought about it. I prayed that my period would come. I often prayed myself into a sweat, but it would be nine long months before I ever saw my period again.

Once the reality of my situation had set in, depression hit me pretty hard. I felt so alone and angry with myself for not sticking to my plans, be-

cause in my mind there was only one way to succeed and that was sticking to my plan of hard work. However, there was a bright spot in my life:
Selwyn. I had not told him about the baby. How could I? What would he
do? What would he think? Would he want to get married immediately?
Did I even want to do that?

I was thinking that I would have to get married and perhaps speed
up my plans for that house. I was thinking that I needed to have a beautiful home to have a baby, but how was I going to do that? I wasn't making
much money and I was still living in a little furnished studio all by myself. I
would sit in my one room with all of these thoughts and just cry. I was so
lost. The mental torment that I was holding in began to manifest itself physically. I became so terribly sick that I needed to tell Selwyn.

I called him when I was certain that there was no turning back and
told him that I was pregnant. His exact response was "Oh, great!" *Oh,
great!* When he said that, I wanted to kill him. I'm sure that was the response that most women in that situation would have expected. I know it
wasn't the reaction I was looking for. So I told him that I was not ready to
have a child yet, to let him off the hook. As soon as I said that, I could almost hear the storm clouds gathering. The fury that came through the
phone was no joke. I feared that, had he been standing in front of me, he
might have attacked me.

"So are you saying you don't want to have *my* baby?" he said.
Somehow he went from "Oh, great!" and not really wanting to have a
baby to being insulted when I said I wasn't ready to have a baby. I was

confused. I couldn't understand why he didn't understand how I felt. After all, he was the one person who seemed to understand and even admire the dreams and ambitions that I had for myself.

"Are you saying that you would be better off not having my baby?" he asked.

I was not sure what kind of mind games he was trying to play on me, but he needed to stop. I was amazed at the selfish, nasty, ego-driven side of this man—a side that I had never seen before.

The man who had put me first in the past was now gone. Not one time did he ask me how I felt about being pregnant nor did he ask if I was okay. None of my thoughts or feelings were even acknowledged by him. I was scared. I didn't have much money. I had $2,000 in the bank and I was trying to make a decent life for myself. That life was rapidly turning upside down.

I wanted him to say, "Okay, we have this baby coming. We need to make a life for this child, so let's get married."

Given the way he had originally presented himself to me—as a mature gentleman—I felt that he would think marriage would be the right thing to do. He made himself out to be an upstanding, responsible, caring person. But that's not who he truly was.

I never brought up marriage and neither did he. When he didn't ask me to marry him, I felt that I had to make a stand.

"I only need you around until the baby comes," I said defiantly to him. I had to let him know that I could do this on my own.

He never asked me another question. He just said, "Yes, okay." I guess I had let him off the hook without realizing it.

My next call after my "discussion" with Selwyn was to Laurice. I told her everything, and when I was done, there was silence on the other end.

"Are you still there?" I had to ask.

"You are?"

"Yes, I'm pregnant."

I knew she wanted to say something more. I could sense it. But she didn't say anything much after that. She seemed to be as stunned as I was about my being pregnant. She said that she needed to see me. I assumed she just wanted to see me in person to know for herself that I was okay. But a part of me didn't really want to see her because I had my own thoughts and fears to deal with. I really felt alone.

Time passed and I had not gone to see Laurice, so she came to my home. Again, she asked me if I had told Selwyn. I told her that I had and gave her all of the gory details that I'd left out. I told her how he'd blown up at me when I'd told him that I wasn't ready to have the baby, and that he'd asked me if I was too good to have his baby. While I was telling her what he had said, I could see the anger growing on her face.

"How dare he speak to you like that!" she said. "What a dirty bastard!"

Then her anger turned to pain. "Voletta, he's married."

I felt my body shake all over. I had never been so angry and shocked. I felt so stupid. And I wanted to kill somebody. Actually, I wanted to kill Selwyn. Married! I felt so used. I felt that he had gotten away with so much. The hate just swelled and festered throughout my entire body.

"Please don't tell him you told me," I said to her as I was fighting back my tears.

The tears were burning my eyes so badly, but I had to hold them back. If I held back the tears, I thought, somehow I would still have my pride. If I had let one tear fall, it would have exposed all the pain I felt for being so naive and stupid. It was as if suddenly I realized everyone could see me in all my nakedness.

I was never angry with Laurice because she'd introduced me to him and knew he was married. She did tell me in the end. She said she'd assumed that he would eventually tell me and that she didn't feel it was her place to say anything. When she'd found out we were getting serious, she said she'd urged him to tell me. But apparently he lied and said that he had told me. And during this period I hadn't spent much time with Laurice. When I wasn't working and going to school, Selwyn had monopolized my time.

Laurice told me that he had an entire family in London, England. He and his wife were supposedly separated. At least that's what he'd told Laurice.

In my heart, I felt and knew that I was a part of some twisted game of his. I guess he wanted to see how far he could take this naive little Jamaican girl. I guess I was his midlife fling. I had been lied to in the worst way and I felt it at my core—that everything I had believed in all of those months was one big fraud. Young people today would say that I had been played.

I couldn't believe what was happening to me; my life seemed to be out of control and everything that could be wrong was wrong. Even in my anger at him I somehow held out hope that this could be fixed, that there was a mistake and he was someone else and maybe he was really separated from his wife and we could make this work. But I knew that I was just lying to myself with that one.

Selwyn was around during my pregnancy. And I'm not sure how I was able to tolerate his presence, but somehow we were back on speaking terms. I knew I wanted my child to know his father.

One day, Selwyn surprised me and said that he was going to take me out for a boat ride. It was a nice gesture and was an opportunity for me to clear my head and have a change of scenery. I remember we went to the top level of this big, triple-decker boat on the Hudson River. We were having a nice time. Every now and then, Selwyn would steal away for a few minutes and then come back to me. I saw him talking to different people and he even introduced me to a few of them.

He had left for longer than a few minutes and I began to get worried. I noticed a man whom I had seen Selwyn talking with earlier. I approached him and asked, "Have you seen Selwyn?"

Not knowing anything about the situation, he answered, "Oh, yes, he's downstairs with his wife."

His wife!

I later found out that his wife had come into town that morning and he'd told her that he was going to take her on a boat ride. After hearing about the wife, I got dizzy. I needed to sit down. When he came back upstairs, I didn't have any words for him. I don't even remember the boat docking and my getting off and finding my way home. But I remember telling Selwyn not to call me again.

"When the baby comes, I just want you to be a good father and take care of your child, but I don't want anything to do with you ever again," I told him.

When I said that to him, he looked shocked. I guess he thought I couldn't survive without him, this small, little girl with nothing. He realized that I had, for the first time, seen him for who he truly was. I may have been the last one to know, but I finally knew.

He gave me some lame excuse about having to take his wife on this boat trip because they were getting a divorce. But it all sounded like a load of shit to me. He kept talking, or trying to talk his way out of it, but I stopped listening.

to know his father

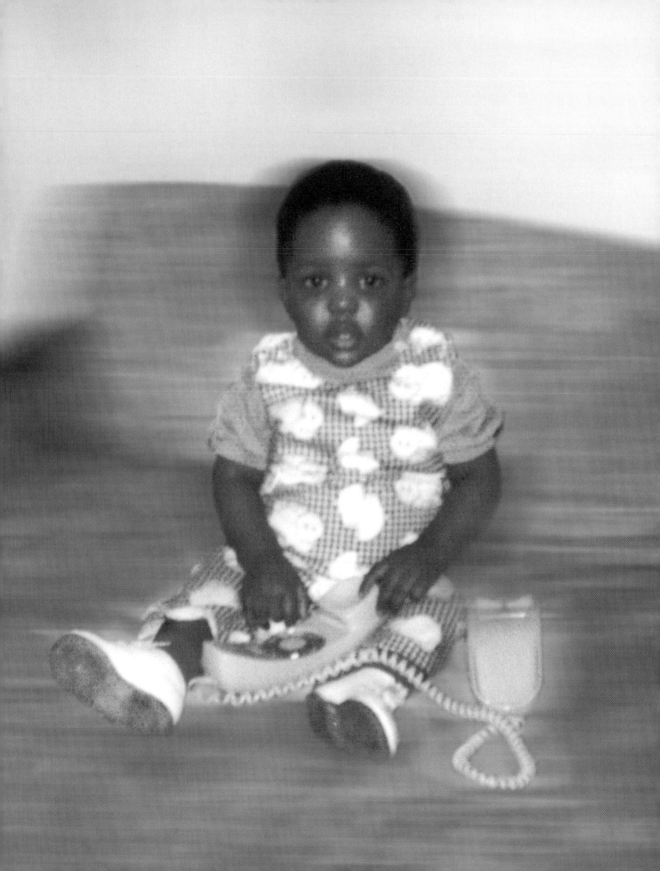

two days before my forty-third birthday

I scheduled an appointment to see my doctor the very next day. He performed a breast exam and found two cysts. He advised me to change my diet immediately. He told me no caffeine, no beef or milk, and scheduled me to come back and see him in one month. I came back one month later, and to my surprise one of the cysts was gone, but the other remained and unfortunately it was bigger and harder than ever. I was sent out for a biopsy two days before my birthday. Two days before my forty-third birthday and I was waiting for the results of a biopsy! Happy birthday to me.

While I was concerned about what could well be the last birthday of my life, I couldn't stop thinking about the most important birthday I had ever had.

37

May 21, 1972. It was early Sunday about one o'clock in the morning. My stomach felt tight and I began to feel a little pain. I called Selwyn and told him that I needed to go to the hospital and that I thought I was going into labor.

"Okay, I'll be right there," he said.

But he never showed up. I ended up falling asleep waiting for him, and when I woke up about two hours later, the pain was back with a vengeance. I called my doctor and told him about the pain I was feeling. He asked me if my water had broken and I told him I wasn't sure. He asked how long it had been since the last pain, and I told him two hours. He told me to call him back when the pain was about an hour apart. I stayed in bed and waited as the doctor had told me to.

Laurice came over and stayed with me through Sunday. She tried to stay with me for the duration, but she had to get up early Monday morning for work. I thought I would have to take a cab to the hospital by myself, but then Selwyn finally showed up—almost fifteen hours after I'd first called him.

"What the fuck is your problem?" My friend screamed at him.

"I knew you weren't really in labor. That's why I didn't come until now."

I wanted to kick him or just hurt him in some way, but I didn't have the strength. I was filled with a baby and a ton of hate. Nine months into the pregnancy and emotionally he was still screwing with me. I was more determined than ever to make a life for myself without him.

Laurice needed to leave and go to work just as Selwyn was coming in. She told him to take me directly to the hospital. She assumed that he would have an excuse not to take me to the hospital, so instead of leaving she said she was going to the hospital with us and she would leave for work from there. He said that I didn't appear to be in labor. Laurice was really angry at this point and said it didn't matter, and that even if it was a false labor, the hospital would admit me. On the trip to the hospital no one uttered a single word. There was complete silence. When we arrived at the hospital, Laurice told me privately that she knew he wouldn't stay with me in the house once she left, and she didn't want me in the house alone on the verge of giving birth.

I was able to walk into the hospital and go straight to the nurses' station. By then my pains were about twenty minutes apart. The nurse on duty escorted me to a room, took my blood pressure, and told me that my doctor was not at the hospital yet but had requested that I be examined. An intern came in to do a full examination, and as I was lying on the examining table, all of a sudden I felt what seemed like two gallons of warm water rushing down my legs. All I could do was scream and ask what was happening.

"It's only your water breaking, sweetheart," the nurse said in a calm voice.

I thought back to the doctor asking me if my water had broken and my telling him that I wasn't sure because I had no idea what he was talking about. I was sick of my own naïveté. *Damn!* That was my water breaking and I didn't even know.

I was in that examining room for hours after my water broke. I was pretty comfortable, experiencing no pain. My doctor came around nine thirty that evening and informed me that he was going to perform a cesarean section because my pelvis was too small to deliver. I was actually relieved by the news because I had heard all of the stories of horrific childbirths and how hard and painful it was. I was actually more scared of going through natural childbirth than a C-section. The way things had unfolded during the pregnancy with Selwyn, I don't think I could have taken much physical pain. I took a deep breath and said thank goodness.

Before the surgery, I was reexamined. The anesthesiologist introduced himself and said that I should start counting backward. The next thing I heard was a distant voice that slowly got closer, telling me that I had a baby boy—eight pounds, twenty-two inches long.

"I made it out, I'm bringin' mad joy.
The doctor looked and said, 'He's gonna be a Bad Boy.'"
—*Ready to Die*, "Respect." Verse 1

■ ■ ■

As I lay there, for some reason my stomach didn't feel right; it felt tight. I was not in pain but my stomach felt strange. I was uncomfortable to the point that I knew without trying that I couldn't get up or even move. I had

baby wallace

breathing tubes in my nose; I had an IV attached to me and all types of monitoring equipment. I asked the nurse what time it was and she told me it was five thirty in the morning and for me to go back to sleep.

When I woke up again, it was about seven thirty in the morning and I rang the bell for the nurse to come because I had to go to the bathroom. She came and brought me a bedpan, but she was busy doing this and that, and she didn't situate me to go to the bathroom. The next thing I knew she was gone and I still had to go. I somehow got out of bed, gathered my strength, and went to the bathroom. But getting off the toilet and back to the bed was more of a challenge than I'd imagined. I didn't know there was a call button in the bathroom, so I just sat there. I guess eventually they missed me and checked the bathroom. I don't know how long I was in there, but eventually a nurse did come and get me.

That entire day went by and I had still not seen my baby. I asked to see him and they told me he was in intensive care. I looked worried. They told me that every baby born by C-section goes into intensive care and that it was normal. I had an explanation, but I still wanted to see my baby. The next day they came to me with papers that needed to be signed before the baby could be circumcised.

I asked again if I could see my baby, and once again the nurse told me I couldn't because the baby had just come out of surgery. By now I was really upset and determined to see my child. I lay in the hospital bed and cried, until I decided that I was going to find out where he was and

has arrived

go see him. I got out of bed and asked where they kept the newborns and I went. When I got to the room, I picked out my baby immediately. Baby Wallace had so much hair it was incredible. He had so much energy, too, kicking his legs nonstop. He was the cutest baby I had ever seen. After seeing my baby I was happy and relieved. I couldn't ask for anything more. With all of the planning, working, and saving, this was the biggest and proudest accomplishment of my life. Nothing was the same for me after that. My focus switched from me. I wanted to do everything for my baby.

I started walking back to my room, and halfway down the hall I just fainted. A nurse saw me falling, caught me, and put me in an empty wheelchair that was in the hallway. I was going in and out of consciousness, but I know she asked me what I was doing there. I managed to tell her that I had gone to see my new baby. She asked me my name and wheeled me back to the nursery window.

"No wonder you fainted," she said. "You just gave birth to an eight-pound baby."

Then out of nowhere with my head ringing, a small crowd gathered around me. The nurse started calling the other staff members over to look at how tiny I was and how big my baby was. I had not gained much weight during my pregnancy, and maybe, just maybe, by the time I delivered I weighed about 125 pounds. After the spectacle was over, they took me back to my room and put me in the bed. I was running a high temperature, and they found out that when I'd fainted, I'd torn my stitches and the incision became infected. The nurse told me that I would not be allowed near the baby as long as I was running such a high fever caused by the infection.

I had so many things on my mind. I often thought about how much of a fool I had been not to see Selwyn for who he was. The thought of him made my entire body numb. The only thing that would have made me feel anything positive was seeing my baby. It had been four days since I'd last seen him, and I had never even held him yet. The nurse knew that I was miserable and depressed because I had not even gotten to hold my baby. I guess she felt sorry for me, so she told me that she would come by and hold the baby up in the doorway once a day until I got better. Everyone in the hospital knew my baby because of how much hair he had, and every morning or afternoon I got to see him. It seemed like forever, but four days later I finally got to hold my baby.

Now I know that everyone thinks that her baby is cute and everyone tells a new mother how cute her baby is. And people will often lie and say that a downright ugly baby is cute. I have seen some ugly babies, and, yes, I'm sure I have said, "Oh, how cute." However, I must say that my baby truly was beautiful.

I decided to name him Christopher because it was a name that I just always loved. His full name was Christopher George Latore Wallace. George was Selwyn's middle name. Despite the anger and disappoint-

my baby was beautiful

ment that I felt toward Selwyn, I wanted him to have a relationship with his son. I never wanted Christopher to disrespect or hate his father on my behalf. I never asked Selwyn how he felt about my giving Christopher his middle name because his opinion no longer mattered to me. My whole life was now about Christopher and me.

I ended up spending eleven days in the hospital, but they weren't nearly as long as the first four days I spent without Christopher.

Selwyn picked me up from the hospital, and when I got home and turned the key to go in the door, I stopped him in his tracks. I told him that nothing had changed.

"I just want you to help me until I get on my feet," I said.

He looked shocked to death, but just as cool as ever he said, "Very well." He made sure to bring me loads of supplies for the baby. I had more Pampers and formula than I could store from time to time. But I'm not sure if he did it for the love of his son or if it was an attempt to resurrect something with me. I guess it didn't matter because the visits to drop off Pampers and other things the baby needed became few and far between. By the time Christopher was two and a half years old, Selwyn had stopped coming altogether.

Halfway through my pregnancy I decided to move out of my small studio and share a large apartment with one of my friends from Jamaica. Julia was eight years older than I was and very experienced. She had four children of her own back in Jamaica.

my life changed

The apartment was a big two-bedroom. I gave Christopher the bedroom and I slept in the living room on the couch. I was comfortable and learning all that I needed to know about motherhood from Julia.

I finally felt strong and secure in my new situation and thought it was time to tell my mother that she was a grandmother. Julia bought me a card, and we took photos and I sent my mother the card with a picture of Christopher. I told her that I was very, very sorry that I had not told her earlier that I was pregnant, but that I had given birth to a happy and healthy baby boy. The card gave her all the details: name, date and time of birth, and the weight and length of my baby.

Gayle and Gloria.

About a month later, I got a letter from my mother telling me all the horrible things that could have happened to me during childbirth. She said that I could have died and that she was all the way in Jamaica and she would not have known. She was upset with me and just went on and on about how wrong I was and why I shouldn't have kept it from her. But all she did was confirm that I had been right not to tell her, for the sake of my sanity. When my older sister, Ruby, got pregnant, my mother cried constantly as if Ruby were going to die. She gave Ruby so much grief. It was as if she knew something that no else knew. I didn't want her doing that with me. Not telling her was one of my better decisions.

Eventually, I went back to work. I was fortunate enough to meet a really nice lady in the building who knocked on my door one morning and said that she watched children and that when I was ready to go back to work, she would love to take care of the baby for me. Her name was Mrs. Phidd.

She was a nice, clean lady who took good care of my Christopher. She was a great cook and even baked him a cake on his birthday. She kept Christopher until he was in nursery school—two years and nine months to be exact.

The only downside about Christopher's staying with Mrs. Phidd was that she had cats. And I found out that my son was allergic to cats. Every day I would pick him up and his nose would be running and his eyes would be itchy and red. I told her that I was going to have to find another babysitter. I never wanted him to experience a moment of discomfort.

Having Christopher changed my entire focus and definitely altered my five-year plan. Before Christopher, I was satisfied with having my GED. But once I had him, I knew that I needed a real career. I didn't have a welfare mentality. I couldn't imagine my child and me surviving off the government and living that way. I somehow knew it was a demoralizing trap that too many young black women fall into. I knew that I needed a profession, not just a job, to give my son the best. I often hear young mothers say that they want the best for their children. What these young women don't realize is that they must make the best of themselves first.

I enrolled in the Brooklyn Training Center. It would be my first step to-

ward becoming a nurse. A woman at the training center told me to come down to the hospital if I needed a job. Inside I knew that I was never going to be a nurse, because working in a hospital and facing death and blood and pain could not be my life's work.

But I had no imagination. My main concern was that nurses were well paid. I just wanted to have a career and get my life moving in the right direction, so I went down to the hospital anyway. While I was

there, I ran into a friend of mine and she told me about a friend of hers who was pregnant and hemorrhaging. The doctors had told her the only way she was going to be able to keep the baby was if she stayed in bed twenty-four hours a day until the baby was born. I told her I could help her.

I ended up working there a few hours a day while I continued to work full-time and take nursing classes. It was a hectic schedule but I had to do it. I needed to provide my son with the best of everything.

He may have been in a single-parent home, but he was going to have the commitment of two people coming from me even if it meant that I worked twenty hours a day.

Finally, the woman's baby was born, but for some reason the baby did not have all of its fingers on one hand. I thanked God that my son had been born in perfect health despite all the stress and torment I had been under during the pregnancy. The woman asked me to stay on after the baby was born. I was willing to do anything that I could to help her out, so I stayed on part-time and went to school part-time. I was doing well in my courses, but I knew I couldn't continue when I saw my schedule for the next semester. A lab requirement would have me dissecting animals. That was it for me. I was tired of traveling all the way out to Queens from Brooklyn, then traveling back to go to work, then rushing home to pick up my son every day, anyway.

I spoke with one of my professors to let her know my situation and that for the rest of the semester I would have to leave early and show up late on most days. She was really wonderful and asked me why I was traveling so far to get to school. I told her that it was the first school to accept me so I had taken it. I had given no thought to the amount of travel, I was just proud to be accepted to a school. Then she asked me what I was planning on majoring in. I told her that I was taking nursing, but that I really wasn't cut out for it.

"What are you good at?" she asked. "More importantly, what do you like to do?"

It hadn't taken me long to know that I was good at being a mother and I liked taking care of young children. I not only loved my son, I enjoyed his company. I enjoyed teaching him and watching him learn and discover new things.

"I love children," I said.

"Have you ever thought about majoring in early-childhood education?" this professor asked me.

In that instant, my life changed. I had a clear focus and direction toward a profession. I immediately transferred to Kingsborough Community College and changed my major to early-childhood education.

I got to see inside a classroom one day when I went to pick up, from day care, the son of the lady for whom I was caring. I got to spend time in the classroom and interact with all of the children in the class.

clear direction

On my way out, the director walked up to me and asked me where I was teaching.

"I'm not teaching anywhere . . . yet," I told her. "But I'm in school to become a teacher."

"The way you got down to eye level to speak with the children, I thought you were a teacher," the director said.

She offered me a position on the spot. It wasn't paying much, so I had to decline. I just couldn't afford to take it.

About a week later I was walking across the Kingsborough campus and my professor stopped me.

"Voletta, I would like you to call this place," she said, handing me a number. "The woman you need to speak with is named Rita Rice. She wants you to call her. Please call her right away, and you may use the phone in my office."

Rita Rice was the same woman who'd offered me a job at the Shore Front Y. She said that she no longer worked there and that she was the new director at the Garfield School and wanted to start a new program. And she wanted me to be a part of it. I was so excited and the money was great. I told my professor and asked her opinion.

"You better take that position, girl!" she said.

It was the most incredible thing to happen to me because it not only allowed me to pay my bills—all of my bills—but also allowed me to work in a field that I wanted to work in. I was also able to keep my part-time job and still remain in school. I enrolled in night school and had a few classes on the weekend. It was perfect. And I got to take my son with me to school on the weekends. It had been so rough for me not being able to see Christopher much because of all of the traveling and things being so spread out and still not having enough money. But everything was finally coming together—I had my career, I was working on my degree, and I was able to spend more time with my son.

Christopher and I were growing up together. I was proud of him and proud of myself, being able to provide for him so well, all by myself.

I had made a conscious decision to have only one child after I had Christopher. I needed to make sure I could take care of him and me. But really, I couldn't imagine loving another child as much as I loved him. And I thought how unfair it would be to that other child.

I doted on Christopher. After paying the bills, whatever money I had left over, I spent on him. I kept him in the most wonderful new clothes. I didn't want him to want for anything—especially food.

The name Biggie, he earned that. It didn't just come out of nowhere. If I had it to do over again, that's one area where I would have done things differently. I would not have fed him so well. But during that time, the mind-set was that the bigger the child, the healthier and happier he or she is. I fed

him whole milk when he got off the formula, and I should have given him skim milk. I used to buy ground sirloin and made sure that he had quarter-pound hamburgers because I wanted him to eat well. I thought I was doing the right thing by him back then.

Education was another thing stressed in our home. Coming from a country where education was expensive and out of reach for most after a certain age, I wanted to make sure that Christopher had the best education. I put him in private schools. It was expensive, but it was the one gift that I wanted to give him because I knew it would be with him the rest of his life. He seemed to enjoy school and was a wonderful student, until he got to high school.

the name...
biggie
he earned it!

MY
BAD BOY

make
the
most
of
my life

"Ms. Wallace, we found something," the doctor told me. "It's a tumor and it's malignant." He told me that I had breast cancer.

I began to think of all the people that I knew who had breast cancer. I could only think of two. And they were both dead. One of the women had been my hairdresser and I don't think she lasted two years after her diagnosis. The other was Laurice. I started thinking about all the possibilities—or lack thereof. I gave myself five years to live. I somehow knew that I would live for just five more years. No more, no less. I had just five years to live and make the most of my life. Five years . . .

I used to watch Christopher sleep every night until he was about five years old. As I stood in the doorway of his room after he had just drifted off, he looked angelic and the same thought always crossed my mind: Can he stay just like this forever? I wished he would never grow up.

55

I remember one evening when he was about ten, he and I were sitting up watching television together. An old movie came on called *Ten Little Indians,* about twelve people stranded on an island who get murdered one by one. As I was watching, I realized the content was a bit too graphic for Christopher and told him to go to bed.

"I think this movie is a bit much for a young boy," I told him.

He went to his room. At about midnight, after I'd gone to bed, I heard this knock at my door. It was Christopher. His chest was heaving and he was out of breath as if someone had been chasing him.

"Ma, can I stay in your room tonight?"

"Of course, sweetheart. But why?"

"I finished watching *Ten Little Indians* and now I can't sleep."

Christopher had a television in his room and had decided that the content wasn't too much for him. But he had apparently had a nightmare and learned the hard way that I was right.

"I told you not to watch that movie," I said.

"I know, Mom. I know," he said as he was dozing off to sleep. "You were right."

All I could do was smile. He was so much more than a son to me. He was my little buddy, my little friend.

Christopher was not a problem child at all. In fact, he was a pleasure to raise. He was kind and gentle and had a wonderful, warm personality. He was headstrong, though, and very, very curious. You couldn't just tell Christopher something. You had to show him. He had to see for himself. He needed to learn by experience, not by example.

I didn't really have any problem with him until he reached high school. That's when he changed. He went from a sweet little boy who loved school to a rebellious youth who hated school. School became the battleground where we had most of our fights.

When Christopher was in the tenth grade, I got a call from one of his teachers one evening. This teacher knew that I was a concerned parent. She knew that I was a teacher and into Christopher's education. I never missed a parent-teacher conference and I was certainly active in Christopher's school.

This teacher told me that she had sent several notes home with Christopher during the past few weeks and assumed I never got them because his behavior had not changed and I had not responded. She was right, I had not gotten a single note, and as far as I knew, everything was fine. But it wasn't. Not only wasn't Christopher doing his work, she said, but he also wasn't showing up for school. All I knew was that he left my house every day with his books and school things. I had no reason to think that he wasn't going to school.

She told me that she was particularly frustrated because they had

warm & gentle

had an exam and Christopher had got a B despite missing most of the material covered. She said he was wasting a good mind. And she said that when he did show up, he was unruly and out of control. The teacher said that during the first marking period Christopher had been wonderful. Then all of a sudden he'd turned into a disruptive monster like the rest.

She said she was trying to calm the class one day and had told Christopher that if he didn't pay attention and get his act together, he would end up being a garbage collector. I think that really upset him. That evening he'd asked me a question out of the blue.

"Ma, how much does a garbage collector make?"

I'm not sure why I had this information, but an article in a magazine listed different professions and their salaries, and garbage collector was on it. It said they started at about $24,000 a year. The average salary for a teacher at that time was about $22,000 a year.

"Ma, do you mean to tell me that a garbage collector makes more than a teacher?" he asked.

Of course, he had taken that information and run with it. The next day apparently he confronted the teacher and said, "If I did become a garbage collector, I would be making more than you!"

The teacher had nothing to say.

"Miss Wallace, Christopher got me," she said. "My point was to make him calm down and pay attention because even a garbage collector needs a little education. But he took it the wrong way. I also used a bad example to make my point."

She wasn't the only teacher having problems with Christopher, I found. And she wasn't the only teacher frustrated that he was just throwing

away work that he had the apparent intellect and ability to do. Another teacher told me, "Christopher seems to come to class when he feels like it." I thought he was starting to go after we had a discussion about it. He said he would start going and I believed him.

But one evening I got a call from the police. They had had a report of a prowler on the roof earlier in the day and found some of Christopher's things—books, notebooks, etc. Apparently he was hiding his stuff on the roof and cutting school and picking it back up before coming home.

I confronted him and it turned uglier and uglier. And he just stopped going to school altogether. I tried everything I could think of. I even had him picked up by truancy officers. I felt bad seeing him in court, but I knew the importance of an education. Christopher didn't grow up in Jamaica, where education wasn't free to all. He only vacationed there. So he didn't fully appreciate what he was getting here.

If only I could make him realize what he was missing out on by not getting an education. As a student in Jamaica I had felt the teachers were too rigid. To put it simply, if a teacher said you were misbehaving, you were going to be punished, and if you were being punished, you were going to be hit, and they usually hit with a belt or switch. I'd never liked the way the Jamaican school system handled discipline because a lot of kids went home each day with welts on their back.

In Jamaica you could be hit for not knowing the answer to a question. I had seen teachers beat students to the point where the child was bleeding from the lashes. I hated it and I knew it wasn't right. But it was a part of my education and it was the norm. Every day I went to school with the dread of being hit and beaten—all of the kids did and I believe they still do in Jamaica.

In the United States, an adult can't even talk too sternly to a child without fear of child welfare authorities being called. And people can march and complain about public education here—and it does need a lot of work. But at least it is a free and open system where children are rarely physically abused. And parents have a voice, if they care to get involved.

In Jamaica, there was no recourse. Parents never complained because if they did, their child could be blacklisted or even made to leave the school. If a child went home and complained and the parent came to the school because his or her child had been beaten across the back until he bled and the cops were called in, that would be the end of the child's school career and the child's age did not matter. In America, it is the law

a child must be educated

that a child must be educated. It's not that way in Jamaica. And worse, if your child is kicked out of school there, he or she is marked for life.

When I was in school, I was scared just to look at certain teachers, and at night I would pray to never end up in one of their classes. I was a really good student and I still managed to be whipped. One day I was in my homeroom class and someone was talking. I didn't hear anyone talking but the teacher did. This was one of those evil teachers whom I often prayed to avoid. He was cruel and brutal and I ended up in his class. And he was hell-bent on dishing out ass-whippings.

There was a routine every day in his class. The bell rang to signal the start of school. Once that bell rang, he insisted on silence while he instructed us on what we were to do that day. Well, the bell rang and it appeared that everyone was quiet as usual. But the teacher didn't start his lecture. "Who was talking!" he bellowed in his deep, threatening voice. In my mind the question was absurd because not a single soul had been talking.

"Who was talking!"

No one answered because no one wanted any part of the beatings he was known to give.

"Since no one will admit to talking, all of you are going to suffer," he said.

We all had to get in a line, and each of us received fifteen licks across the backs of our hands. It was painful. He was kind enough to give us the option of getting the licks on our hands or on our backs.

It was so infuriating because I knew I wasn't talking, and I hadn't heard *anyone* talking. I was fourteen years old then but I still remember it as if it were yesterday, that's how hard he hit me—how hard he hit all of us. He beat me across my hands so hard that I had bruises and lumps all the way up my forearms. I couldn't take it. I had to turn around and let him finish beating me across my back. I hated him until the day he died.

Recess was fun but I dreaded most of my classes, especially one of my serious reading classes. We read all the classics such as *Gulliver's Travels* and *A Tale of Two Cities*. I had no problem with the reading, but the questions that you had to answer (or not answer) in front of everyone—those were my problem. I knew that this particular teacher made it his business to try to humiliate students. So even if I knew the answer, it was tough because he made me so nervous I could hardly get the answer out. Sad to say, but school was just not fun for me in Jamaica.

When I arrived in the United States and went back to school, it was a different story. It was a real pleasure for me. I enjoyed learning. I enjoyed the exchanges with my teachers and my classmates. During one of my first weeks in school, the teacher asked a question and I knew the answer. I stood up—as I had been taught to do in Jamaica when answering a question—and everyone looked at me as if I were crazy. I didn't know that you didn't have to stand, which was a sign of respect (and not standing before responding in Jamaica meant a whack across the back). When I started teaching, I had a Japanese mother who came and bowed to me and said, oh, thank you, teacher. I thought she was crazy, but I soon real-

a sign of respect...

ized she was honoring me and giving me respect because I was going to be the one to educate her child about the world.

I learned quickly and enjoyed every minute of it. And even with all I had going on, working and raising Christopher, I always looked forward to going to school.

School in America is such a privilege. Far too few American students really appreciate what they have. I was most saddened that my own son, who'd watched me work hard to get through school, had such a lackluster attitude toward school. It was one of my most painful moments with my son, realizing that not only didn't he like school anymore, but he might actually drop out altogether. I never imagined that my own son would be taking his education for granted. But that's exactly what he was doing. And he was doing it in grand fashion and getting worse.

He was not only cutting up at school, but he started bringing that attitude home, as well. He would bring his friends to the house, and when I would come home from work, I would hear so much noise and commotion coming from his room that I had to do something. The noise was incredible. There was loud talking and then loud music, then loud talking and then banging on the furniture. I would say to myself, "My God, what the hell is going on in my house?" I remember one day in particular it was really getting out of hand.

"Whatever you are doing in there, you will knock it off right now!" I yelled outside the door of Christopher's room—which was always closed.

music MUSIC...

Christopher came out of his room and said, "Ma, please calm down. We're just practicing."

"Practicing? Practicing what?"

"Music."

"That is *not* music! That's noise."

He went back into the room and I heard him tell his friends to quiet down. Later, after they'd left, he came to me and said, "Ma, when I'm in my room doing my thing, do I need to get a lawyer to do it?"

"Christopher, do you know music?" I asked.

I didn't know anything about rapping at this time, and I couldn't conceive that the noise he was making in his room was any form of music. What I did know was that my son could not sing. In my book, he had a lousy voice. So I told him, "Yes, you definitely need a lawyer."

He realized that he could no longer practice his "music" in my house. So he started going across the street to someone's basement and did his music over there. Soon after, when I would look out the window, I began to notice huge crowds gathering across the street. It was like some kind of party. I could not imagine that Christopher was at the center of all that. It seemed that everyone on the block was gathering in a small basement just to hear him rap and do his "music" thing.

Just a couple of years before all of this rap business, Christopher had still been very much my little boy. I'd sit on the stoop and watch him play childlike games with his friends. I wouldn't let him out of my sight.

his music thing

And when he got really restless and wanted to run wild, I took him to the park.

When Christopher was thirteen or fourteen, he still had boundaries. He knew he had to be in before it got dark. His curfew was eight thirty. And he hated it with a passion because all of his friends would still be outside until about eleven. But I never believed that any child should be staying outside any later than eight thirty or nine. Nothing good happens after those hours—especially to teenage boys.

Eventually, it all changed. And he just started feeling that he was a big man and could do what he wanted. And he was getting too big for me to make him do what I wanted. And it wasn't that I was ignoring what he was doing, I simply didn't know all that he was up to. I just knew that I had dreams for him and my dreams weren't his dreams.

I always wanted him to commit himself in the classroom and finish school. I knew Christopher could be so much more. That's why I sacrificed to put him in Catholic school. And for the first few years he was doing well—bringing home A's and B's. But he decided all of a sudden that he didn't want to wear the uniform. He ended up at Sarah J. Hale High School and then Westinghouse High School in Brooklyn. He was assigned to a dental lab when he started there. They told me he was doing so well that he could get a scholarship if he stayed in school and maintained a B average. But he wasn't interested in school.

He wanted to be onstage. He wanted to be a rapper.

Before completing the tenth grade, at the age of seventeen,

Christopher dropped out of high school. I knew he was never going back to school. We battled over this for three months. He cried and I cried. He cried and I cried some more.

Then he stopped coming home.

He was not an adult and legally I was still responsible for him. So I filed a person in need of supervision (PINS) warrant. I had to go to court and spend the whole day there with a bunch of other sad people. I felt like a criminal. That made me so angry that I left that courthouse in tears, that I had to go through all of that just to get him off the streets. Finally, after many days, Christopher called me.

"I'm telling you right now, the cops are looking for you," I told him. "The cops are going to arrest you when they find you. Either you go to school or don't come back to my house."

Regularly, to the point where he was finishing my sentences, I would tell him that if anything happened to him on the streets . . . he would jump in, "I know, Ma, you're going to be a rich woman."

He thought he was real wise with that, but I knew one day he would understand when he had his own children.

He went to school the next day but spent the weekend at his friend's house. When his friend's mother found out Christopher was there without my permission, she called and apologized.

He came back home with a letter in hand. He could write letters that would just melt your heart. In this letter he apologized and promised to do better. He went to school and for a while he was doing well. But then the streets started calling again. He started hanging out with a gang that called themselves Junior M.A.F.I.A. And he was talking about doing that rap stuff as a career.

Music to me was what they played on LITE-FM. I was actually a country music fan. I liked the twangy rhythm and the words that always seemed to tell a story. But one morning I was up really early. LITE-FM had a lot of static for some reason, and I turned to a clearer station and ended up on HOT-97. They were playing Toni Braxton's "Breathe Again," and I thought it was such a beautiful song and that she had such a lovely voice. The next song that came on was a rap song, and I was about to turn it off but the voice sounded familiar.

"Ba-by, ba-bay!" the voice crooned. And I said, "Oh, my God! That is Christopher! And he doesn't sound bad, either."

But I knew there was no way that it could really be Christopher. It was five in the morning and he was still asleep in the next room. I listened to the whole song, and when it went off, the radio personality said, "That was Super Cat with Biggie Smalls."

Christopher at age ten

I made a mental note as I was drifting back off to sleep that when I got up, I would ask Christopher if he had anything to do with this Super Cat person. I was on my way to sleep when another song came on and someone named Da Brat said, "How you living, Biggie Smalls?" and then this voice began again with the rapping. That had to be Christopher. I couldn't take it anymore. I needed to know right then if it was him. So I ran down the hall to his room and banged on the door.

"Christopher, get up!" I yelled.

"Whazzup, Ma?" he said, still dazed from sleep. I asked him if he had done music with Super Cat, and he said yeah.

"What about this Brat person?" I asked.

"Yeah."

"Christopher, are you really making music?"

"Look, Ma, I told you this is what I wanted to do."

"So you're serious?"

"Yeah, Ma, I'm serious."

That was enough for me. I walked back to my room thinking how in-

smiling proud...

credible he was. I went back to bed but I couldn't really sleep. I just lay there, smiling, proud as can be. Then I heard a knock at my door. It was Christopher. I told him to come in.

He sat next to my bed and was real still. "Ma, I know you worry about me. I know you went to college and got your degree and you're working. And I think you did real good for yourself and for us. But that's not for me right now. What I'm going into with this guy, I know can make a lot of money. He told me that he can make me a millionaire by the time I'm twenty-one. And, Ma, I want to pursue it.

"You know I can't be you. I cannot pursue what you have pursued. Ma, I need this for me. You want me to be a decent citizen. Well, this is the thing that can allow me to be that decent citizen."

I couldn't argue with that. After we had that conversation at five in the morning, I never switched the station from that day. HOT-97 became my station, and every time I listened I heard about Christopher and his latest project, CD, or sound track he was working on. I heard him with this group called Total. He was doing something with a Mary J. Blige. He was doing something else with a One Twelve. I remember thinking, "Wow, he is really going to make it!"

I didn't and I couldn't understand for the life of me how that noise he was making in the room with his friends was going to translate into money for him to support himself as an adult. But just like the teacher in his classroom so many years before who had challenged Christopher and ended up speechless, I was left speechless. Christopher left me speechless. He showed me that my way was not the only way that leads to success.

While I still wished that he had even a hint of desire to finish school, I had to be satisfied that he was doing positive things with his life.

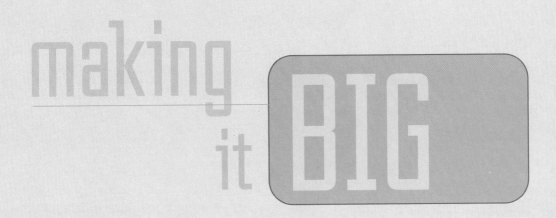

HE WAS NOT READY
TO DIE

5 years to get my affairs together

I don't know anyone diagnosed with cancer whose first

few thoughts were about the good china and where the

silverware was, but those were the thoughts running

through my head when Dr. Elsworth told me that the lump in

my breast was indeed malignant, that I had cancer. I had just

turned forty-three and my son was just becoming an adult.

While I thought I would have five years to get my affairs

together, I wanted Christopher to know where everything

could be found and what was of value. I wanted him to be

completely prepared.

I left the doctor's office in a daze, my mind spinning.

What should I do first?

I knew my next conversation after leaving the doctor's office had to be with Christopher. I needed to prepare him for what was going to happen to me. I didn't know how I was going to live out the rest of my life, but I knew that I had to tell him. I came home and sat him down. I didn't know where to begin, so I went straight to it:

"Christopher, I have cancer."

He wouldn't even let me finish the rest of what I had to say. He put his hand up and said, "Ma, I don't want to hear that!" He got up and left the table and went to his room. Every time I tried to bring it up, he would cry and walk away. He was so angry and hurt.

I didn't want to tell him about the cancer, I wanted to tell him about death.

"Look, I have a lump in my breast and it's not good," I said to him when he finally came out of his room. "It's cancer."

Tears just streamed down his face and he sat in complete

silence. It hurt me to see him like that, but I am and always have been a realist.

"Mom, you're going to live," he said. "Now, come on. I don't want to talk about this."

And the conversation was over. We never spoke about it again.

Ten days after finding out I had cancer, my former boss and friend went with me to check me into the hospital. She always seemed to be there for me during a time of need. We drove there in silence. She didn't know what to say and neither did I. But she was with me the whole time and that felt good. The next morning, the doctor had already informed me, I would be undergoing a radical right mastectomy. That's when it became real to me. I had cancer and this was serious.

My whole outlook on life had changed right there in that cold, sterile doctor's office. My head began to pound. And I was someone who never got headaches. I started having chest pains. And while I was certain I wasn't having a heart attack, I knew the stress from dealing with this bad news was about to kill me—if the cancer didn't.

The day of my pre-op testing, the nurse took my blood pressure. It was normal, but before she left the room, she said, "Let me tell you something. What you are going through is enough to make anyone's pressure high. But I know one thing: if you have something in your life and it's a bother to you, get rid of it!"

Her words helped me. It gave me an image and a sense of empowerment. I didn't feel like a victim. I felt that I was taking action against

outlook on life

something that was bothering me. I felt a little in control, at least for a while. But that feeling left when I returned to my hospital room.

I remember sitting on the bed, my arms sweating. I didn't know what to expect from the surgery—except that I might not make it out of there. *I'm going to die.* That's what happens to people with cancer, isn't it? I sat on that bed thinking about my mortality and how quickly my life would be ending.

An intern walked into my room to go through the basics, taking my blood pressure again and temperature. I looked at him and thought how young he was. He looked no older than twenty, not much older than my own son. How much he had accomplished in a short time, I thought. I wondered if I would live long enough to finish school, to see my son through school or get a GED, to see him married with children and successful in the career that he worked so hard at.

"What is your worst fear?" the intern asked me.

The question took me off guard. I tried really hard to answer him, and though in my head I was telling him everything, nothing would come out of my mouth. I just started crying. In between the sobs, I managed to calm down enough to tell him that my worst fear was that the cancer had already spread.

"You know, you're a young woman," he said, looking at me. "Don't think the worst."

That is all that I remember him saying because once again my brain shut down with an overload of fear and panic. The intern was still talking but I wasn't hearing him. I just curled up in a ball after he left and drifted off to sleep. Later that evening the nurse came to help me put my things away. She was a real pleasure, with a warm demeanor and a hearty laugh. She was joking with me because I'd packed so much stuff, as if I were moving in, she said. I even had dental floss.

Early the next morning as they prepped me to go into surgery, a lot of my family and friends showed up to support me. My little room was full, but it didn't matter. While I appreciated the support, I was alone in my own troubled world, all alone. My sister Melva, who had moved to the United States a few years before, was there. She had so much fear in her face that I didn't want to look at her. I didn't need to see that. She stood far from me, but it was as if I could read her mind. She was afraid that I might die, and she was afraid that she, too, might get cancer. I could feel all of her fear and hear all the thoughts coming from her. It was so strange a moment, but I could just feel it. My uncle Burke was there, too. As they were rolling me to the operating room, he was in the doorway, and I could see his tears; he was the last person I saw before going into surgery.

In the operating room I remember everything being really bright. The lights were almost blinding. I glanced over just as the doctor was putting the IV into my arm and I was told to begin counting backward.

The next time I was conscious was hours later. And my first thought was *I am awake and I am alive!* I knew I was definitely alive because I had never experienced so much pain in my entire life. They anticipated that I would be in pain because as soon as my eyes opened, the nurse rushed to my bedside and put a control in my hand that would allow me to administer the pain medicine as I needed it. I was in shock, but that was superseded by gratitude. I was grateful to still be alive. The fear of thinking that you're going to die is exhausting, and I couldn't tell what hurt more, my body or my mind. I remember my friend holding my hand and trying to distract me from my pain, telling me something about a tunnel on which to focus. She was great.

The next day, the same young intern who'd examined me before I went into surgery walked into my room smiling. He looked around and told me that I was someone who is loved a lot because he had never seen so many flowers in one room. The strange thing is that I don't remember even seeing them until he pointed them out. There were flowers from my family in Jamaica and from all of my friends in the States. There were even flowers from the eighteen students in my class. It's funny how fast news can travel, because I had only told one of the parents and, of course, my principal about my condition, and I had flowers and cards from each and every student in my class. My mood was certainly lifted.

The doctor began to explain to me that my surgery had been successful and that my lymph nodes were clear, free from cancer.

"We checked twenty-two, and they were all cancer free," he said.

While I was excited, I had to ask, "Well, how many lymph nodes does a person have?"

"About twenty-two."

The weight in my stomach had been lifted and my brain began to thaw. I didn't want to hear him tell me that they had checked twenty-two, but that twenty remained and there was a chance for it to spread. I didn't have much hope for myself as it was, but whatever hope I had I didn't want to give up without just cause.

While the worst seemed to be behind me, my rehabilitation began a few days after surgery and put what used to be ordinary movement of my arm into perspective. Every inch of movement was excruciating. But I often thought of Christopher while I was doing my exercises. Christopher had not been to the hospital and I understood. I was glad that he had his work to keep his mind off the fear of losing me to cancer. While the masses saw my son as this big, hard man, I knew that underneath that overwhelming exterior was still a scared little boy. My little boy.

My cousin Sylvia, who was a registered nurse, was always at the hospital with me, and she asked if Christopher had been to the hospital yet because she hadn't seen him. I told her no. She didn't like or accept any reason for Christopher not being there. She called him on his cell phone while he was at the studio. She told him that he should come downstairs right now because she was sending a car for him. When Christopher got to the hospital, he just looked around. I could see it wasn't his kind of place.

"I was afraid to see you because I didn't know what you would look like," he said. "I didn't know what I was going to see."

He didn't need to say it because I already knew. He settled down and didn't really have much of a reaction to how I looked. I'm sure I looked a little better than he expected. He sat with me for quite a while and didn't leave the room once, not even when his phone began to ring. He sat in the chair next to my bed and handled the business with whomever he was talking with on the phone.

When I came home, I was feeling good, but I had to continue the rehab until I had full range of motion in my arm. I was fortunate that I would not have to undergo chemotherapy—my doctors put me on tamoxifen, which is an oral hormonal treatment. Just being able to avoid chemotherapy gave me a great deal of hope. I looked forward to going home and getting back to work as soon as possible. Christopher was a big help when I did finally get home. He came home every single night until I started back to work and made sure that I took my medicine and worked on my rehabilitation daily.

After remaining home for nearly five months, I went back to work in July to teach a few classes and started back officially in September. Going back to work helped me tremendously. Walking into that class that first morning was memorable. One of my students, upon seeing me, just started to cry. I wondered whether I looked different or whether she had just panicked because she hadn't seen me in such a long time. I wanted to pick her up and just hug her, but I couldn't. I guess I had lost a step or two physically, but my personality and love for the children were still there.

That first day back also opened my eyes to the fact that I wasn't alone in this fight against breast cancer. My assistant informed me that the teacher downstairs had had a double mastectomy and another staff member had had a lump removed. It felt good to be in the company of so many survivors. And it felt good that I, too, was a survivor.

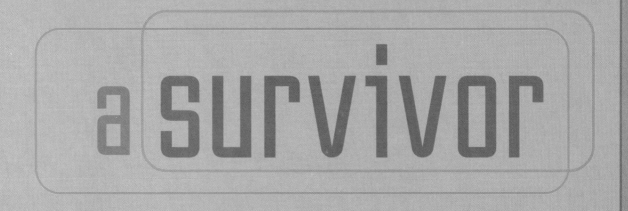

a survivor

MY
BIG POPPA

THE HAND

The hand, small, comforting, gentle
and soft

Cuddling, precise, warm and giving

It welcomes, rebukes, denies, and
destroys

The hand, huge, cold, silent, unmoveable

It's LOVE, it's HIS, it's GONE, it's not
FORGOTTEN

Life has become more valuable

Given a second chance at life, I wanted to experience every-

thing good and do it to the fullest. Life had just become more

valuable than I was ever able to express with words. This is

why despite Christopher's new mess, I was going on my

annual trip to Jamaica, and instead of my usual fourteen days,

I was going to spend twenty-one days.

Not only was Christopher getting into his music, he was also becoming somewhat of a ladies' man. So many girls were calling the house and coming by that I lost count. One girl in particular, Rose, seemed to be coming by regularly. She was from the neighborhood, but I didn't really know much about her except that she seemed much older than Christopher and seemed friendly. I wasn't surprised that she was older because I remember when Chris was about fifteen, maybe sixteen, one day he and I were in the house and he said, "There is a girl coming over, and if she asks you my age, could you tell her that I'm twenty?"

I was so curious. I wanted to see this woman who was going to come into my house. I needed to know whom I was going to tell that my son was twenty when he was only sixteen.

The bell rang, and for the first time for as long as I could remember, his room was immaculate. I said nothing. I just waited and he escorted the woman to his room. I walked to his room and the door was closed and I heard a little voice inside the room saying to my son, "Oh, you are so spoiled. You have everything in this room." I opened the door and walked in and said, "Hello, I'm Christopher's mother. Do you know how old he is?"

She was shocked. She looked at me and then at Christopher, I'm sure wondering why I would ask her such a question. Shaken, she said, "Biggie, what are you doing?"

"Excuse me," I said. "That is a sixteen-year-old kid."

such a loyal person

The woman almost had a heart attack. She turned to him and said, "Biggie, what are you trying to do to me!" He said nothing and she got up and ran out of my house apologizing profusely.

So Christopher was up to his old tricks with the girls as far as I was concerned. To this day, I don't recall the first time I met Rose, something I find strange because she has a very recognizable face. She just always seemed to be around. Every time I looked up, there she was in my house.

Miss Thang was friendly enough but she was there too much for my taste. At one point, I thought she had moved in. I finally had to say something to Christopher. In my usual style, and especially after all that I had been through with my health, I didn't have time to sugarcoat any of my thoughts and feelings.

"Christopher, she needs to go," I said. "Call it a motherly instinct, but that is not the girl for you."

Those were my exact words to him. I couldn't explain why. I just got a bad vibe from the girl. I didn't feel that she was bringing anything to the table, and I didn't feel that she could enhance his future. She wasn't ambitious enough for Christopher. But Christopher said that she was *his* girl. No matter what I said, he was loyal to her and said they were going to be together.

I recognized that he wasn't looking to defy me; he was just being loyal to Miss Thang. I have never met a more loyal person than Christopher.

Before long, he and *his* girl seemed to be having problems. It seemed as though they were having them from the beginning. They broke up and got back together for what seemed like a hundred times during one year. And I didn't like it.

I guess I'm old-fashioned, but I didn't want them in my house alone, and I certainly didn't approve of their having sex. I told Christopher that he was too young to have a steady girlfriend, and that having a so-called adult relationship while still living in his mother's house was unacceptable. I couldn't understand this silly teenager in front of me talking about "I'm in love." He didn't even know what real love was about.

Then one day Rose approached me with, judging from the look on her face, some really sad and disturbing news. It was after one of their fights and she needed to tell me something important. I'm here to say that one man's sadness can certainly be another man's glee.

"Miss Wallace," she said, "I want you to know I love you very much, but Christopher and I won't be seeing each other anymore. I just want to say good-bye." And she hugged me!

I was screaming *Hallelujah* at the top of my lungs—in my mind anyway. I was never happier that two people had decided to part ways. And while I wanted the best for her, I wanted that best to be far away from Christopher. I knew that she could do a lot more with herself and for herself than to sit in the house waiting for Christopher to come back from doing whatever he was doing at the time. She needed to develop herself in every way that is important for a young woman mentally and physically.

Not to mention that Christopher needed to do some maturing of his own. I could think of no better way for them to work on themselves than apart. To top it all off, her downfall was insecurity.

But my glee and relief didn't last long. One afternoon Christopher bounded into my room and said, "Hey, Ma! Guess what? Rose is pregnant!"

What! I didn't need to ask if he was serious, although he was quite a practical joker. I just knew it was the truth if for no other reason than it was the last thing I wanted to hear.

"Well, is it yours? And are you getting married?"

"Yes. And no."

"Can you afford a child?"

"No."

"Well, then, keep that child away from me." I meant it.

If he wasn't working, wasn't going to school, didn't seem to have anything financial going for himself, I wasn't taking on the burden of a child. I knew he was rapping, but he wasn't signed to any label yet so he didn't have any income at all, as far as I knew. I was in a real defense mode. I wanted to live my life and enjoy it without undue stress. I was not going to allow it. I was just not going to accept it in any way. I knew with all of my being he was not going to saddle me with the responsibility. So I decided right then and there I would rather not see the child than to be put in that situation.

Christopher made a move toward responsibility. Mr. Christopher got a little job packing bags at the Met Grocery on Fulton Street in Brooklyn near our home. He also told me he was working as a courier, and supposedly this courier job paid well, but he would still be living with me.

A few months went by, and I'm sure the question I'd asked him when he'd first told me about the pregnancy was finally eating at him. And Christopher, being a realist himself, went to Rose and said, "My moms wants to know if that's my baby." She assured him that it was.

That was good, but it didn't matter to me because I wouldn't be seeing the child, anyway. I was preparing to go on my three-week trip to Jamaica. The morning before I left, I got a phone call. It was Rose's sister. She told me that Rose was in the hospital. I guess they couldn't find Christopher. As far as I was concerned, there was no decision to make. I was not missing my plane. I left Christopher a note with all the details.

When I came back from my vacation, Christopher was sitting in front of the building waiting for me.

"I have a little girl," he said.

Christopher's face was beautiful. It was lit up with pride. I was still on defense, determined to keep my sanity and my freedom, determined not to allow myself to be saddled with a child at this stage of my life.

"Ma, I want you to meet this little baby."

I turned to him with all the strength I had in my heart and said, "Christopher, keep your baby to yourself! I don't want to meet any baby."

He was absolutely relentless, he kept begging me, "Ma, please,

please see this baby. Please come see my baby. She's the cutest thing."

"Chris, I'm sure she is," I said. "And, no, I don't want to see any baby. Are you still working? I hope you're still working, because babies need things. They are very costly."

He didn't hear any of that. He just said, "Ma, please come see the baby."

I fought the good fight, but I gave in and went to see the baby. I complained all the way to Rose's house. I was pissed for reasons that the two of them together couldn't understand. I was angry with them for being so irresponsible and bringing an innocent life into this world that neither of them could take care of. They had no right to do this. It wasn't fair to anyone. But here I was on my way to see this new baby, a baby that I hadn't even thought of as my grandchild yet because I couldn't get past the anger.

Christopher called ahead to let them know I was coming. He knew my mouth when I was angry, and he was right. It was certainly best to warn them that I was on my way over. When I got to the house, he led me to a room that was all the way in the back of the apartment. When I got to the room, the first thing I saw was the crib, and I walked toward it real slowly, not sure of what I was going to see or how I would feel. I looked in the crib, and all I saw was this little, tiny thing like a ball in blankets with a tiny face sticking out, and I fell in love instantly. I started crying.

That moment felt like the first time I'd laid eyes on Christopher. I

give her the World

didn't think it was possible to duplicate that overwhelming feeling of love that I had had for Christopher, but I was wrong. This was *my* grand-daughter that I'd lived to see, and right there I knew that I wanted to give her the world. I wanted her to have everything. She was the daughter I never had and I was going to see that she didn't lack a thing.

Ma Rose and Pa Chris didn't have dry shit in their ass to give that baby. I forgot that it wasn't just the baby and I alone in the room. When I looked up at Chris and Rose, I could only roll my eyes at them in disgust. I didn't know what the future would hold for the baby. It was such a dirty, rotten world out there, but I knew I wanted the best for her.

Christopher snapped me back into the present. "Oh, my God, you're not crying, are you? She's not *that* ugly!"

Christopher always knew how to break the ice, and comedy was his greatest tool.

I picked up the little bundle. It was feeding time and I wanted to give her her bottle. I fed her, put her back in the crib, and walked out of the tiny room. The image of her in that little room made me cry for days.

The next day Christopher brought little T'yanna to my house. She spent the night and slept in my bed. And she hasn't left my bed since. T'yanna would spend every weekend with me. I made a room for her in the house, bought a bed for her, made sure I had Pampers and baby food on supply. I was doing the very things I said I would never do. But I couldn't help myself. I loved her to death. And all was well again between Christopher and Rose. I was settling into my new life as a grandma with the baby.

Then things started to go sour. It seemed to happen all of a sudden. Christopher started paying more attention to that rap thing and spending more and more time in the streets. And Rose started wanting more and more of Christopher's time. They were constantly fighting, and Rose started threatening him with not seeing the baby. They even fought in my house— screaming, pushing, and they even broke one of my expensive lamps. Before I knew it, all three of us were in my living room fighting and screaming at the top of our lungs.

"Somebody owes me a goddamn lamp!" I said. It was so ugly.

It was the beginning of what would be the ultimate end of them as a couple. Looking back, I can see Christopher and Rose couldn't have made it long-term. She was too insecure and jealous. If they were ever going to have a chance, she would have needed to get a life of her own. She would go out in the streets, practically following him wherever he went. She felt that she needed to keep an eye on him.

She was really creating a lot of problems for herself and Chris. He would go to the studio, which if you know anything about recording, means ungodly hours between midnight and dawn. That's the norm. But it didn't matter what time Christopher got out, Rose would be there waiting for him and ready to fight any women that might be in his presence.

I wished that she would have gone back to school and finished her education and got a career going or just set some goals for herself. It seemed that Rose (and Chris) ran from education like the plague. She would have fared better had she not built her life around him. That's no way for a person to live. I wanted her to be a better example for her daughter. At the same time, I wanted Christopher to continue working on his dream. I didn't want him to be stifled or stopped in any way because of Rose. I saw for the first time in Christopher's life that he was focused and energized, and I wanted him to take it as far as he could. The energy that he was putting into his music career made me proud. I just quietly wished that he could have put half as much into his education.

It was frustrating to watch and listen to the arguments that they continued to have. He would tell her, "Look, I'm trying to make it happen for us!" And knowing Christopher, I knew he was telling the truth. He was loyal to his friends; how much more so would he be to the mother of the child he cherished. But she couldn't see it. They broke up five months after T'yanna was born. Nevertheless, he took care of his daughter, and the relationship he had with his daughter continued to blossom. He called her his little TeeTee.

Not long after his relationship ended with Rose, things really started taking off for Christopher. He had a recording contract and two managers—two men that I got to know really well—Mark and Wayne. Christopher started coming home with money—real cash—and his music was getting airplay.

Christopher had his first hit single, and it was time to shoot a video for "Juicy." He asked me to be in the video. I was really reluctant because, while I was proud of him and all that he had done so early in his career, I didn't want to be a part of that whole rap scene. It was not something that I felt represented me. I found the rap scene to be a bad example of a good time for young people with all of its decadence and showiness. It was a real dilemma for me, so much so that I went to my elder at the Kingdom Hall for advice on the matter. He told me that I needed to do whatever settled my heart. It was a matter of conscience.

So after a whole lot of soul-searching, I agreed to be in Christopher's video. The deciding factor for me was when Christopher said, "There is no reason for me to hire an actress to play my mother when my own mother isn't dead!" So I played his mother in the video.

On this hot August day, I was supposed to be coming out of a car wearing a full-length mink coat. Instead they shot the first scene in my house, turning it upside down.

After tearing up my house, they cleaned up and had a Lincoln Town Car waiting for us to go to the Hamptons to complete the shoot. It was me and T'yanna on the two-and-a-half-hour drive to the Hamptons, and I was glad to be going. I wanted to support my son.

I had never been there before, and as we pulled into town, all I saw were palatial homes and beautiful mansions. This was the world I had dreamed of so many years before—*this* was my vision of America.

In these dream scenes, I had been dressed in beautiful clothes and pretended to live the life of luxury. I had no clue what I was getting into. Here we were shooting a video in the Hamptons, among the wealthiest people in the world.

Mark, Christopher's manager, always told me, "Ma, he's going to be big one day, really big." And I would say, "Oh, please! He needs to finish school. If he wants to be big, he needs to go to school."

I had to admit that Christopher was doing well for himself. Perhaps he was getting a different kind of schooling, one that, though it couldn't benefit him the way real school could, was certainly giving him the kind of life he'd always dreamed of. Maybe he did have it all figured out after all.

the life he'd always
dreamed of

love is...
love
graceful...
peaceful...
respectful

"LOVE" IS

Presentation of love is love Eventful

Application of love is love Delightful

Supplication of love is love Graceful

Demonstration of love is love Thoughtful

Construction of love is love Skillful

Affirmation of love is love Fruitful

Duplication of love is love Peaceful

Adoration of love is love Respectful

97

With everything going so well—fame, money, success—I knew it was too good to be true. Just when I thought I could relax and sit back while Christopher enjoyed his new life, in usual Christopher fashion here he comes with a bombshell.

I had come home from work and Christopher was sitting on the steps of our building. It seems he just loved to sit on those steps and shock us with his stories. As I walked up to him, I noticed he had a strange look on his face.

"Christopher, what's wrong with you?" I asked.

"I did it."

"Did what?"

"I just got married."

"You're married!" It was too much for me. I was annoyed. "Christopher, every other week you're 'in love' with another girl. How in the world did you decide you needed to get married!"

Girls were constantly calling the house for him—even then. He was getting more calls than customer service at the phone company. Now he was telling me that he was married. I was convinced that he didn't want to be married, and furthermore I thought there was no way that Christopher *needed* to be married. So I decided that he was lying. I didn't say another word to him about this so-called marriage. I went into the house and pretended that he had never spoken those words to me.

I'm not sure if I gave what he'd said a second thought. But he followed me into the house and wouldn't let up.

in love

"Ma, I said I really got married today."

I still did not believe my son was married, and he knew that I didn't believe him. I must not have been the only one, because he followed me up the steps into the apartment saying, "No one believes I got married."

There was no more talk of marriage.

A few days went by and I got a call from my sister. She was hesitant to talk, which was not like her. She was beating around the bush about why she'd called, then finally she came out with it.

"Is Christopher married?"

I was a little unnerved but I asked her where she'd heard that.

"Well, I just heard him on the radio sending shout-outs to his wife, Faith."

His wife? Faith?

After I hung up with my sister, I called Mark, Christopher's manager, and asked him if my son was really married.

"Yeah, Ma, he's really married," Mark said. "She's a nice girl, too."

"Well, do you really know this woman?"

"Yeah, I met her and she's a real nice girl."

I needed to speak with Christopher when he came home. Yes, he was still living with me, which further led me to believe he was lying. What married man would be living home with his mother—without his wife?

When he came home, I was waiting for him. "Christopher, how long have you known this woman that you supposedly married?"

"Oh, about two weeks," he said nonchalantly. "She's a cutie, so I had to lock her down."

"Do you have a picture of her so I can see what your wife looks like?"

He pulled out a picture of her and handed it to me.

"Is she white?" The woman in the picture was so fair-skinned, I wasn't sure. She looked Caucasian to me.

He fell out laughing. I hadn't seen him laugh so hard in a while.

"No, Ma! She's black."

"She *is* pretty."

"That's what I told you."

While he was living with me, he spent most of his time in the studio, and the women were still calling and leaving messages. One evening the phone rang and I answered it. The voice on the end sounded familiar—as if

this person had called on several other occasions but had never identified herself. But on this night she did. She said her name was Faith.

"Faith?" I asked.

"Yes."

"Are you the Faith that's supposedly married to my son?"

"Yes."

By my tone, she could tell that I wasn't necessarily pleased to hear from her. In fact, I was a bit annoyed with her.

"Honey, how would you feel . . . No, how would your *mother* feel if you just went off and got married and this husband of yours kept calling and never acknowledged your mother and never identified himself?" I asked. "I bet she wouldn't like it. You have called here several times and not once did you say 'Hello, Miss Wallace' or 'How are you, Miss Wallace? This is Faith.'"

"I know, Miss Wallace. You are absolutely right. But it's not my fault. Christopher told me to stay away from you."

"What? Am I hearing you correctly?"

married to my son

"Yes. He told me to stay away from you. To be honest, I would feel the same way that you do. I understand. But please don't blame me."

I was so mad and so hurt that I think I might have hung up on her. I went right to Christopher's room, banged on his door, and didn't wait for him to respond.

"Why the hell did you tell this girl to stay away from me! What the hell am I, a monster?"

Christopher looked me right in the eye. "First of all, you weren't supportive of this marriage and you know that. Ma, I love you. But I love my wife and I did not want her to come around here and for you to insult her or disrespect her because I did not want to have to choose between my mother and my wife."

It was a strange moment for me because I understood why he did what he did. And I thought he was nice and thoughtful to think that way. At the same time, I wanted to slap the shit out of him for keeping her away from me that way.

I spoke with Faith on the phone on Saturday, and Sunday she came to the house. My friends were all there, and Christopher officially introduced her to me as his wife. I welcomed her into the family and told her that I was glad to finally meet her.

After she thanked me, she said, right in front of Christopher, "This should have happened a long time ago. That's Christopher's fault that it didn't."

He just smiled and walked away.

christopher

The two decided they needed to live together. So Faith and I began to look for a house for them, but it didn't pan out. They settled on a nice duplex apartment in Brooklyn that I was proud of. Things seemed to be going well for them.

She had signed a recording contract before Christopher. And her first album, *Faith,* had been released. Actually, she had had a career writing music before she even got signed as an artist, so she was doing well when she met Christopher. But her star rose even higher when she released her own album and was crowned the First Lady of Bad Boy.

But as usual, when things are going well, something bad always happens. During this time a whole bunch of controversy starting popping up surrounding Tupac. He got shot in New York while going to a recording studio where Christopher happened to be with Puffy working on a CD. There was speculation that my son and Puffy knew something about it, and it was one big mess.

Prior to this, Tupac and Christopher had been friends. Tupac used to call my house often asking for Christopher. But then it got nasty and somehow Faith got mixed up in the middle of it and the press just had a field day.

And in the midst of all of this, my second grandbaby was on the way. Chris and Faith had officially broken up. And I guess during a brief reconciliation they had had time to make a baby. That put an interesting spin on everything.

The pregnancy and the pending birth of my grandchild calmed things for a while. I was on my way to Bible study when I got a phone

jordan wallace

call from Faith asking me to call Christopher because she was having labor pains and would need to go to the hospital soon. So I put a call in to him so that he could meet her at the hospital. Once again, another call, another baby!

I told her that I would call her as soon as I got back from study hall. As soon as I got back, I called her, but there was no answer so I knew that she had to be at the hospital. The next day, my boss drove me to the hospital. Christopher was there but was in a wheelchair because his leg was broken. He had broken his tibia in a car accident he had had with Cease, a rapper and member of Junior M.A.F.I.A.

A week before, a police officer had hit the handle of Christopher's truck, knocking it off, in a minor swipe. So Christopher's truck was in the shop. They had a rental car, which Cease was driving, and as they were heading around the curve onto a ramp leading to the New Jersey Turnpike, Cease ran into a guardrail. The car was pinned and Christopher's leg was broken. He was on crutches and in a wheelchair for months. In fact, the first time I saw him walking was in the "Hypnotized" video, and he had a cane then.

When his son was born, Christopher showed up at the hospital in a wheelchair. He didn't seem to be angry or depressed about being stuck in the wheelchair. He just took it all in stride and accepted it. He even joked in one of his raps about how Lil' Cease had crippled him. Christopher took everything for a joke—even that accident.

By the time I got to the hospital, Faith had already delivered the baby. She was up and looking healthy and the baby was in his unit—the nurse brought him soon after I arrived. He was beautiful. He didn't have a name yet. And Faith and Christopher asked for my help in the naming.

I was really happy about helping to name my grandson. The first name I came up with was Charles, my father's name. But they didn't like it. They said it sounded too English. Then we thought about John, but Christopher thought the name was too plain. So finally I said, "You know what? I love the name Christopher!" And we all agreed. Christopher was a fan of Michael Jordan's, so he thought about Michael for a middle name, then decided on Jordan. And that was it: Christopher Jordan Wallace. I don't know how long we spent looking at the baby and naming him, but we were in our own world.

I changed little CJ's diaper, and he was already circumcised—I put bacitracin on his incision. We stayed in the room together for hours, just taking care of the baby. Even though Faith and Christopher were having their problems, for that day we were a family again. Faith was the wife of my son. I respected her and loved her.

Having gone through my battle with breast cancer and being worried about Christopher's future, this day I was truly happy because I knew that no matter what, Faith could take care of everything. I knew she loved Christopher and that if I closed my eyes the next day in death, Christopher had found someone to love—even if they didn't stay together.

I don't know how strong the relationship was after the baby was born, but there seemed to be a pattern. By the time T'yanna was born,

Christopher and Rose were no longer together. And he and Faith didn't last long after CJ was born.

Their relationship broke up because too many people were involved in that marriage—too many of Christopher's friends. They did not want his marriage to work. They didn't want Christopher and his wife to bond. They wanted Christopher all to themselves, and Faith was in the way. Someone was always pulling him to party or pulling him to a club. Everyone was taking him away from the marriage. They were jealous and he didn't even realize what he had at home with Faith.

Christopher and Faith never got to grow into husband and wife. It was amazing to see how his friends would show up at their home in droves and have him back on the streets at all hours of the night. It still makes me sad to think about it because the marriage could have worked. It could have survived if Christopher was not surrounded by such selfish people, who only had their own best interests at heart.

I'm glad I decided to stay away and not be an overbearing mother-in-law who poked around in their business or tried to make decisions for them. When the marriage ended, I never said, "I told you so!" Even though I knew my son was not ready for marriage. He was not mature. He had no idea what a real marriage would take, and his friends were not the types to encourage him to explore the possibility. It seemed that the more success he gained, the less attention was paid to the things that were truly important.

the more **success** he gained...

the less **attention** he paid to the things

that were **truly important**

ON THAT
MORNING

another
long
day
for me
at
school...

I was tired. It had been another long day for me at school, and while Christopher wrote that I pimped an Acura with a mink on my back, nothing could have been further from the truth. I didn't even drive then. I still don't. I just never learned how.

Christopher had settled into his life. He was separated from his wife but he was coming into his own. His first major purchase was a beautiful home in Teaneck, New Jersey. While he wanted me to move, I had no aspirations to do so. Despite its horrible reputation, which my son had helped contribute to, Bedford-Stuyvesant was not an evil pit in the heart of Brooklyn. For me it was home. It was where I'd raised my son and where I knew everyone else in the neighborhood.

Another long day had brought me home tired and looking forward to the weekend.

I was sleeping hard when the phone rang. It was exactly four thirty in the morning. I couldn't really make out the voice on the phone at that hour. I would have bet it was a wrong number. I was so tired and groggy I couldn't even make out what the person was saying.

Who is calling me at such ungodly hour?

Once I realized the babble and confused talk wasn't a prank, my senses came to me. The person was calling my name and crying so hard he could barely breathe.

"Who is this?" I demanded.

I had to repeat myself because I don't think he heard me over his own crying.

"Who is this?"

"Miss Wallace . . . Miss Wallace . . ."

I finally recognized the voice. It was Damian, one of Christopher's friends. *Damian!* What was wrong with him? I knew it had something to do with Christopher. But the way Damian was acting was scaring me. I screamed at the top of my lungs for him to answer me, but the response didn't come soon enough. I was sitting up in bed, screaming into the phone asking for him to tell me what had happened. My sister-in-law, who was staying with me, came rushing into the room and took the phone out of my hand.

The words came out of her mouth in slow motion. It was finally beginning to register for me. Each word came out like a blow to my chest, knocking me off my feet and back onto my bed. I heard "Christopher" and "killed." I was in shock. I didn't know what to think or what to do. But I knew that I needed to know every detail.

When my sister-in-law hung up, I called L, Christopher's best friend, who was also living in New Jersey at the time. I told him that Damian had just called and told me that Christopher was shot and killed.

The words were more than L could handle. He also screamed at the top of his lungs. "No! Miss Wallace, don't say that!"

He told me that he had gotten a call earlier that morning at about one, saying that there had been a shooting in Los Angeles, but they hadn't said that Christopher was hurt.

"Look, give me a minute," L said. "I'll get back to you as soon as I find out what's really going on and what really happened out there."

I called Rose, T'yanna's mother, to see if she had heard any of the madness. And if it was true, I needed to be near my granddaughter. When I told Rose what I had heard, she was at a loss for words and like Christopher's best friend, L, couldn't believe it either. Rose wanted to know more, but I didn't have any more to tell her. She started crying so hard and just kept saying, "Miss Wallace, stop telling me this. Please don't say that."

Then I thought about Faith. I had to call Faith. I knew that she and Christopher were no longer together, but she was the one person who came to mind whom I felt I could trust. And more important, I knew she would be there to support me through all of this.

be there for support

Everyone that I had called kept telling me not to say what I was say-ing, as if I wanted to say that my firstborn and only son might be dead. As if I wanted that to be true.

I called Faith. I didn't care if Christopher and she were enemies at the time. I knew Faith and I knew she would be there for me. She was the woman whom my son chose to be his wife. She was the person I had grown to trust.

I called her cell phone and there was no answer. I left a message. I don't think more than ten minutes passed before she called back. When I learned that she was already in Los Angeles, I was happy because that meant she would be able to get to the bottom of everything. She would be able to find out what was going on with Christopher.

"Miss Wallace, I know there was a shooting, but I'm here and I don't have any details," she said. "I will find out as much as I can and do my best to keep you informed."

By then, friends were piling into my home, and denial was my whole self. I chased them all out, but they stayed around for support.

Christopher's business partner was able to book a flight to Los An-geles almost immediately. Quicker than I could pack and before it could really sink in exactly why I was heading to the West Coast, I was getting on a plane at Kennedy Airport to Los Angeles. I wasn't alone. Rose, Money L, and Mann were with me. T'yanna was with her other grandma.

my firstborn my son

I didn't speak a word during the entire plane ride. I passed in and out of consciousness—knowing but not believing that Christopher was dead. Someone offered me a drink that I might have wanted, but I wasn't able to respond. My throat was so dry, so hard and tight, that it was physically painful. I did attempt to speak twice, and each time nothing would come out. I didn't drink or eat the entire time. I just thought about Christopher. *Christopher.*

He and I had practically grown up together. I was so proud of him. He always tried to make things right. He always seemed to know how. Christopher was uncomfortable if he couldn't make things right. Who was going to be there to make things right now?

I remember one day I had come back from a dentist's appointment only to find half the things in my apartment gone—the TV, the VCR—everything that could be carried was gone. They had broken into my apartment from the fire escape through the kitchen.

I could not rest after that happened. I was scared every time I came home. If only I had an idea of how scared I should have been. One afternoon I fell asleep in the living room on the couch and woke up to find that my entire place had been robbed again. It was official. It was time to move. I had had every kind of security feature installed, including bars on every window, but still I had no comfort. I didn't want to go in my house alone, and I didn't want to stay in my house alone. I was scared just going up the steps in the afternoon when I came home from school.

Shortly after the second robbery, Christopher came running into my room. He had been at the West Indian Day Parade all day—so he said.

"Ma, you would not believe what happened," he said when he got home. "The guy who robbed you was shot and killed at the parade today. He tried to pickpocket some man and steal his watch, the two started fighting, and the man pulled a gun on him and shot the robber dead right at the parade."

"What!" I said. "That sounded just like the man who robbed me—bold as ever. He came in and robbed me while I was sleeping, looked and saw me and kept robbing the house with no fear of being caught!"

I was glad that Christopher hadn't been hurt during that shooting, and I was glad that the crazy, relentless thief was no longer around to terrorize me in my own home.

About a year later Christopher and I were in the car with one of my friends. We were going to the Aqueduct Flea Market. I was telling my friend about the back-to-back break-ins that had happened to me and how I was robbed by this guy while I was right there in the living room sleeping on the couch.

"Wow!" my friend said in shock. "You must have been horrified."

I told him about how that fool had tried robbing the wrong person and how he got too bold and ended up getting himself shot to death at the West Indian Day Parade the year before. I told him how the robber had tried to steal someone's wallet and watch in broad daylight, and how the man had killed him and it served him right. As I

alone

was telling him, I heard, "Quack, quack, quack!" in the car. It was Christopher.

"Why are you laughing?" I said.

He was laughing so hard, he could hardly breathe. He couldn't even answer me.

"Christopher!" I said. "What is the matter with you?"

"I was only kidding," he said.

"What!"

"You were so afraid, Ma, I had to do something. You couldn't even go up the stairs by yourself. So I had to tell you that so you could forget about that nigger and stop being afraid to live in your own house."

"It's not right playing with life like that. This is not a joke."

"Ma, you've been sleeping at night and going upstairs to the apartment by yourself, right?"

I wanted to give him a hard punch, but the truth was he had fixed the problem. I was not afraid of my home anymore. Christopher knew me and he just had a way of making it all better. He was about seventeen at that time.

I managed a faint smile now, thinking about my crazy son. As the plane taxied in, I was glued to my seat, eyes staring off. I was so isolated in my thoughts of me and Christopher that I didn't even realize that we had landed. As the doors opened, my chest was so heavy. It felt as if a piece of lead were lying on my stomach. As people crowded to leave the plane, my nerves were just shattered. Nothing seemed right. I felt alone and scared.

and scared

People were waiting for us when we arrived in Los Angeles. Everything was a blur and I preferred it that way, because on every terminal television I could hear and see breaking news with pictures of Christopher with a caption underneath: "Notorious B.I.G." I could hear the newscasters say his name, "rapper Notorious B.I.G." I was doing my best to drown out all of that. I was still holding out hope that whatever they were saying, they had it wrong. It would not be real until I saw for myself.

Damian and Lil' Cease were the first people I remember seeing that day. A lot of other people were there, but their faces blended into the background and the names I don't remember. So many people had gathered together, many of whom I had never seen before, crying and mourning. I believe they must have been fans of my son's. I saw grown men crying, and I even saw people laughing at the men who were crying, which was a distraction from my own thoughts. Perhaps the other guys were laughing because it was strange seeing such big men breaking down like that and they didn't know how to respond.

I don't know who started the whole macho thing with all of the unspoken laws about how men are supposed to respond. Grown men aren't supposed to cry? Why not? I knew too many young men who were dead because they felt the need to prove how macho and manly they were.

Once outside the terminal, I was driven to a hotel. I had no idea where I was, but when I got to the hotel, the streets were jammed with an unbelievably immense crowd. Police officers were everywhere.

As I was walking toward the hotel, one of the police officers stopped me and asked to speak with me. I couldn't imagine what he wanted. I had just arrived. I kept walking and he asked again to speak with me.

I turned to him and said, "For what? I just got here. You know more than I do. I still don't know the true status of my son. I should be asking *you* questions, I should be asking *you* to shine light on the situation for me."

The cop said nothing else. He handed me a card and said, "If there is anything else you need, please call." And he backed away and blended into the mass of people outside the hotel.

Finally, I got inside the hotel where Christopher had been staying. I asked for the key to his room. I wanted to see his room. I needed to see his room. What I was looking for, I didn't quite know. I entered his room slowly. I didn't want him to startle me too bad. I was expecting Christopher to come out of the bathroom and say, "Hey, Ma! Is that you?" I was expecting this to be one of his practical jokes.

wanted to see his room

DESPAIR

I walked silently to his room, waiting to hear his voice:
Hi slim, mom dukes, mommy dearest, Ma!!

Instead I heard the steady flow of central air.

Each moment I stared, and listened, wondering, where
is he?

How is he? Is he in pain?

Was he in pain?

Did he get a chance to think, to wish, to hope, to call out,
to cry out Ma!

I heard something. . . .

The thud of my heartbeat,

The quiet flow of my breath,

I HEARD NOTHING.

I continued looking and listening for anything that would indicate that Christopher was still alive. But the only sounds that I heard were coming from the air conditioner and the faucet dripping in the bathroom.

The first thing that I saw that belonged to him was his bag at the foot of the bed. As I got closer, I saw his tuxedo was spread out neatly across the bed. The room was filled with Christopher. It was as if he had stepped out for a second and would be coming right back.

I continued to just look around and listen, and in that total silence it hit me. In my mind I admitted for the first time that Christopher was dead. For a minute I felt scared and maybe a little out of control because I was alone. But I knew for certain that Christopher was not coming back. All I could do was sit down on the bed next to his things. It made me feel close to him.

Out of nowhere the phone rang, shaking my already fragile nerves and destroying what felt like my last bit of quiet time alone with my son. I picked up the phone and it was Faith, telling me that I should come to her hotel because it was safer there. She said it was best for me not to be alone among all the chaos that was surrounding Christopher's hotel.

I stayed in the room a little while longer. I wasn't at all afraid that something would happen to me. I felt relaxed. I felt that it was our last chance to be alone together without the world watching. It felt like it was our quiet time together the way it used to be when he was growing up and it was just me and Christopher. I used those minutes to come to grips with the reality I knew waited for me once I turned the knob to leave the room. I knew on the other side of that door were the media floodgates, the questions. There would also be so many lies mixed in for good measure.

I needed to have complete control over my emotions before I walked out that door.

Rose and I took a cab over to Faith's hotel. She had CJ with her and I was so happy that my grandson was there. There are no words to explain the warmth and comfort I got from playing with and holding that little boy. I looked at him and saw innocence. He was a breath of fresh air from all that was going on. I was happy that he didn't know what was going on around him. I was happy that he didn't have to feel any of the pain and anger that was around him. To this day, I thank God for sending me that little bit of comfort and light through my grandson.

Rose and I shared a hotel room that adjoined Faith's room. I didn't get any sleep that night because I was up with people from New York making funeral arrangements. Rose's presence also helped, but she had to leave early in the morning. I wanted her to be at home with T'yanna because I had to stay in L.A. I didn't want T'yanna to hear from the television or from anyone else what had happened to her father. And her mom had told her just that. They would not keep her away from the television much longer.

Faith and I really got to bond while I was in L.A. We received a lot of flowers while at the hotel. We gathered all the flowers and left them at the scene of Christopher's murder.

our quiet time

When I did finally get some sleep, it was not restful. I tossed and turned all night. I remember just sitting up in bed and Faith would come in periodically to check up on me. On one of her checks, she had some news for me.

"Miss Wallace, my friend just called me from New York, and she said that it's all over the news that you and I are out here in L.A. fighting. Can you believe that?"

I was almost too weak to respond. How ridiculous. I just hoped that T'yanna was being kept away from the tele-lies.

"You know something, Faith?" I said. "I wish we were fighting, because it would mean that I had some strength and that I would be able to feel something other than what I'm feeling now."

We both laughed at the scene and the fools they were making us out to be back in New York. It was the first time I'd laughed in two days. People can be so cruel.

The next day a car came to pick us up and take us to the coroner's office. I asked to see Christopher's body. They said that we could not see his body because his death was the result of a crime and it was under investigation. So they gave us a picture of him, which showed him from the waist up.

The picture did not look recent. It wasn't a picture of him recently dead. It looked like a picture of him just out of surgery after the car accident he had had on the New Jersey Turnpike. I remember the picture because I was at the hospital that day and it was the only time he had been hooked up to an IV.

What in the world was this photo doing in Los Angeles?

It would be the beginning of an infinite number of questions that I had regarding my son's murder and the so-called investigation. The Los Angeles Police Department was doing a lot of questionable things and telling outright lies. It seemed to me that they were not truly trying to solve this murder or get to the bottom of it.

According to the reports and eyewitnesses, Puffy's vehicle was in front of Christopher's. Trailing my son's SUV was the security SUV. So I learned that behind my son was a car that had the job to watch out for Christopher and his safety. Basically it was there to keep an eye on him.

But for some reason, no one in the security vehicle saw a car pull up next to the SUV that Christopher was riding in and open fire. Not only could these security people, who might have been off-duty Los Angeles police officers, not identify the shooters, they couldn't even identify the vehicle. And why didn't professional instincts lead them to pursue the culprit or even get a license plate number?

If these security guards were veteran cops, why didn't they have the instincts to call 911? They didn't report that someone in a vehicle had just been shot at. Instead they drove past Christopher's SUV and pulled up next to Puffy's to tell him what had happened while my son was in the SUV dying.

Upon questioning during the so-called investigation, none—not a single one of those cowards in that security vehicle—came forward to tell what he saw. There are just too many damn questions that need to be answered.

8:00 p.m.

The night began at the Peterson Automotive Museum on Wilshire Boulevard in Los Angeles at a party hosted by Vibe magazine, Qwest Records, and Tanqueray gin to celebrate Friday night's eleventh annual Soul Train Music Awards. The guest list was a who's who of the East Coast hip-hop world, including Busta Rhymes, Heavy D, Da Brat, Jermaine Dupri, and of course Notorious B.I.G. and the head of his label Bad Boy Entertainment, Sean "Puffy" Combs.

9:30 p.m.

According to sources, the party really got going between 9:30 and 10 P.M. Biggie appeared to be having a great time, taking a table near the dance floor and chatting with friends. According to a witness, there was no discernible concern about being in Los Angeles on the part of anyone in the Bad Boy group despite the so-called beef between the East Coast and West Coast.

12:35 a.m.

The party becomes overcrowded, and as is often the case in such situations in Los Angeles, the fire marshals were called and the party was shut down.

12:40 a.m.

A large crowd formed outside the venue, with people pouring from the party into the parking lot and onto the streets. There were valet cars, stretch limos, and luxury SUVs waiting and further clogging up the streets.

12:45 a.m.

According to published reports, Biggie and Puffy were outside the club, talking to friends about going to another party. Puffy had his car brought around and drove off. Then Biggie and two friends—reportedly, Lil' Cease from Biggie's group, Junior M.A.F.I.A., and Biggie's bodyguard, Damian—got into his GMC Suburban. Biggie was in the front passenger

12:45 a.m.

side. The Suburban, according to reports, pulled up to a red light at Wilshire and Fairfax, then another car, described as a black Jeep, according to the *Los Angeles Times,* pulled up to the passenger's side of Biggie's Suburban and fired six to ten shots.

1:15 a.m.

Biggie, whose real name is Christopher Wallace, is pronounced dead at Cedars-Sinai Medical Center.

While I was pondering all of the unanswered questions and the great mysteries surrounding my son's death, I still had business to deal with concerning his burial. It was time for me and my son to go back home to the East Coast. The plane ride from Los Angeles was much worse than the ride coming. We flew Christopher's body back to New York on the same flight that we were on.

I thought about the trips that Christopher and I had taken to Jamaica every summer since he was a little boy. Those were good thoughts because they took me away from the heart-wrenching thought of him lying in the belly of the airplane. I kept thinking of him underneath me and it was ripping my heart to pieces. Everyone worries about his or her expensive luggage and wants people to take extragood care of their Gucci and

sitting in silence

Louis Vuitton bags. But my cargo was my son. And the image of him below just stayed with me the entire trip home.

Once again, for the entire trip I sat in silence. There was no way I could turn and explain that I didn't want him down there. On the ride back I just held on to memories of CJ real tight. I slept most of the way but he helped me get through that plane ride. When the plane landed, the record company requested that we stay at a hotel for a few days, then Faith and I decided to stay at Christopher's house in Teaneck, New Jersey, where I finished making the funeral arrangements.

It was time to bury my son. On that morning, two cars came to pick us up and we rode together, Faith and I, to the memorial service. It was an open casket and I allowed Wayne (Biggie's manager) and the rest of Christopher's people to select his suit. It was a great help to me that they had the suit designed by Flavor Unit 501. I didn't get involved one bit with how they dressed him because I knew they would do right by him. I only stepped in when they wanted to bury him in his Rolex watch. I thought we were putting enough in the ground as it was.

March 19, 1997: Frank E. Campbell funeral home on the Upper East Side was filled with the hip-hop elite, from Mary J. Blige to Public Enemy, Queen Latifah to Salt-N-Pepa. They were there to pay their final respects to the King of Rap.

Biggie's body, in an open casket from the waist up, was clad in a white, double-breasted suit and matching hat. After the ceremony, his body was placed in a hearse and driven from Manhattan through his old Brooklyn neighborhood of Fort Greene. Thousands of his fans flooded the streets, climbed onto cars, and hung from buildings to catch a glimpse of his hearse. The crowd was rowdy; they brought the noise. It was the kind of response Biggie had gotten in concert. It was a fitting farewell.

a fitting farewell

IS IT

MO MONEY,
MO PROBLEMS?

he would
sit on
the edge
of the
bed &
we would
talk

Christopher had been working late at the studio and meeting

with people all day. It was about two o'clock in the morning

when he came in. He had a routine when he came home. No

matter what time it was, he would call out for me to see if I

was asleep. If I was awake, I would call him into my room and

he would sit on the edge of the bed and we would talk.

129

Usually it would be lighthearted talk—just chitchat about his day

or his dreams. And then he would go off to bed. It was almost as

if talking to me helped him sleep better.

On this particular evening his steps were a little slower, his

demeanor less light.

"Ma, this business is worse than a serious drug game on the streets," he said.

I felt so much stress coming from him. I could only console him like a mother and tell him that everything was going to be okay and that things would get better. He just smiled and patted my hand.

Looking back, I'm sure he was thinking that I didn't have a clue about what he was talking about. And he was right. I didn't know a thing about the "music business." And I sure didn't know anything about the "drug game" either. I gave him the only advice I knew to give him—don't give up and keep moving and eventually everything will work itself out.

I didn't know then—and never in my wildest dreams could I have imagined—that I would one day know and understand firsthand what the hell he was talking about. Christopher's death brought a lot of revelations. It changed a lot in the way I viewed the world around me.

I loved teaching. It wasn't just a job for me. When I started teaching in the 1970s, it was the culmination of a lifelong dream and I loved everything about it. I looked forward to going to school every day. I couldn't wait for September. I would get butterflies just thinking about the first day of school and the new children and watching them grow throughout the year as they picked up knowledge. It was real. I could see before my eyes the result of my hard work. When a child who was struggling finally got it, I could hold on to that. I got into teaching for that feeling—the feeling that I could make a difference in a child's life.

That feeling was the motivation behind my getting up every day. It was why I believe I recovered from cancer. The thought of being there for Christopher coupled with getting back to my kids at school helped me beat breast cancer the first time.

I used to hear people complain about their jobs and talk about how they hated going to work. I couldn't relate. I looked forward to just going to the classroom and seeing the kids smile. They were beautiful and made my day. These were two- and three- and four-year-olds. They would share their little lives with me, and some of them had sad stories and I would comfort them. I loved and cherished their innocence.

Every year after the kids were gone the principal would call me into the office and say, "Oh, Voletta, your class is already full for next

love teaching

September." All of the parents of children who left my class would tell the next set of parents, "Make sure you get your child in Voletta's class." They said I was the most patient teacher in the school. And it happened that way every single year of my teaching career.

I could never get bored with teaching, if only just because of getting to know all the different personalities. Oh, there were certainly times when I wanted to strangle some of the kids and there were some stressful days. But overall the kids were wonderful.

One little boy in my class was named Benjamin. His mother came up to me one day after school and said, "Voletta, my whole family was over for Thanksgiving and Benjamin asked for you. He said, 'Where is Voletta?' I told him, 'Voletta is at home with her family.' He said, 'Why? How come she's not here? I thought you said she was family. She's supposed to be here.'"

PROSPECT PARK
Y M C A
NURSERY SCHOOL
1994-1995
NEARLY NURSERY

Another little boy used to wake up on Saturday mornings and say he was going to school, his mother told me. Little Aaron told her he needed to go to school to see me.

Teaching was a big part of my life. One of my favorite times of the day was Monday morning before school started. I would come in about an hour early to set up the classroom for whatever project we were going to work on for the day. Then I would hear these little footsteps rushing toward the room around five minutes to eight. And that's when the day really started—with big hugs and kisses, as if they hadn't seen me the Friday before.

I would get these wide eyes and the stories of the weekend—everything from the shopping trips some took to the fights some of their parents had. I used to have to remind the parents that they must watch what they do in front of the kids because children remember everything and have no problem repeating what they see.

"If you discuss your personal business in front of your child, I will hear about it, and if you have a fight over the weekend, I will definitely hear about it," I would tell them.

My lessons extended beyond the classroom and beyond my kids. I also tried to inspire and motivate the parents to be their best. I got complete satisfaction and fulfillment from teaching.

my life

But I lost my desire to go back when Christopher died. I tried to put on the good face and continue teaching, but my heart wasn't in it. I'd left my heart in a Los Angeles street in a hail of bullets.

I had to stop. It just wasn't fun anymore. When the kids would come in and give me hugs and kisses, I wasn't feeling it. I guess it meant something all of those years because I also knew that I could go home and have the same thing. These kids weren't a substitute for anything, but an addition.

But after Christopher was killed, the hole was so big that nothing could fill it. I couldn't muster the affection for my kids. I couldn't reciprocate any of the affection the kids gave me, and when I did, it wasn't genuine. I was in too much pain. I would often find myself in a daze staring at the kids, and somehow I would be transported back to when Christopher was their age and I would relive a moment.

Going to school was becoming torture. It was torment being around the children and watching the parents with their children, realizing I no longer had my Christopher. I would think that they had all of this time with their children and I was left with nothing—my son's life was cut down, cut short. My son's life was silenced.

It was getting to a point where I would dread Monday mornings. That's when I knew what I had to do. I still loved the children. I loved them enough to know that they didn't need a halfhearted or brokenhearted teacher. They didn't deserve that. They deserved 100 percent of me each and every day. It was time for me to leave. Thirty-one years, cancer, ups and downs, my own struggles raising my son—none of that had made me question leaving. Not once.

The murder of my son forced me into retirement.

The first Monday that I didn't return to the classroom, I decided to take care of some business. I cashed in my retirement benefits, I cashed in my life insurance policy, and I collected on the policy I had taken out on Christopher when he was fourteen years old.

A lot of people have the notion that "Biggie" left me a lot of money and made me financially set for life. And while I did eventually inherit a lot of money from his legacy, I had already taken care of myself before I saw a dime of that money.

While Christopher was alive, he worked hard and made a lot of money. I never lived vicariously through him. All of those rap songs about what he'd bought me were more bravado than anything else. He didn't buy me a car because I never knew how to drive. I worked as if my son weren't making money.

I was officially retired. Retirement for me would be time to heal and move on to the next stage of my life, which I imagined would be writing children's books. Little did I know retirement would not mean a time for me to relax at all. I learned that managing my son's estate would become a full-time job. I not only inherited his money, but I inherited his friends and "bitches"—both male and female—especially the friend who referred to herself as the Queen B.

I left one school to go to another—Music Business School. The world that Christopher had thrived in that I'd purposely kept at a distance I was now thrust into. Shortly after Christopher's death, I got a crash course in contracts, conflicts, and royalty rip-offs. The hardest thing for me to deal with was not all of the legal stuff, it was the people. I didn't have a clue about how I was going to navigate through all of Christopher's people.

The first thing that I learned in Music Business School is that everyone—and I do mean everyone—is out for himself. Everyone is looking to take advantage of anyone he can. If money is involved, you can and will be raped and robbed of it until you and the money are no more.

Shortly after Christopher's death I decided to write a book. It was going to be my therapy. I was introduced to a young man whom I will only call Mr. Rip Off. He said he would help me write my book and get it published. We met and he interviewed me on several occasions and we spoke for hours. When he was done interviewing me, he told me that he needed several thousand dollars as his fee to complete the project. I gave him the money that he asked for, and I haven't heard from him since.

This was a so-called reputable writer, a published author. I was appalled to realize that someone would go to such lengths to swindle someone out of even the smallest financial reward.

It would be the first lesson I learned in the business, that a person's word is worth no more than a wooden nickel.

the king of rap

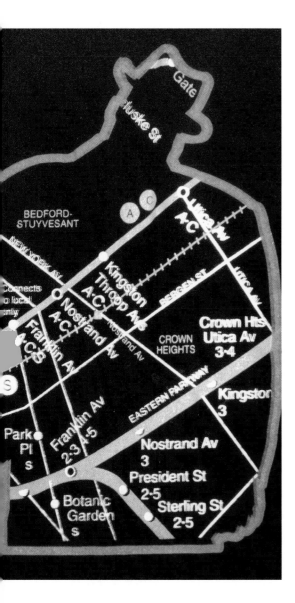

Shortly after my son's death, Christopher was being praised by most people for his work. He was even labeled the King of Rap. At his funeral were some of the biggest names in the music business. And when his hearse rode through the old neighborhood, you would truly have thought a king had died—with the out-pouring of love and emotion from his fans.

Those who were interviewed following his death had Christopher's name at the tip of their tongues with all kinds of accolades and praises. And some seemed to use Christopher's death as an opportunity to squeeze themselves into the spotlight. One name and face that continued to surface was Lil' Kim's.

I was interviewed after his funeral, and the reporter asked me what I thought about Lil' Kim being at the funeral. In truth, I didn't care or think anything was wrong about Kim being at the funeral. As far as I was concerned, she was there to grieve like everyone else. She did have a legitimate place at Christopher's funeral—as legitimate as that of anyone else who knew him.

I can't say I remember seeing Kim at the funeral—not that I remember much of the day. It was all a haze for me. But later that evening, she was all over the news, being held up by Mary J. Blige. Kim seemed to be in a lot of pain over my son's death. Shortly after, she did an interview and I heard her explain what my son meant to her. She said that Christopher was her mentor and she loved him to death.

I remember the first time I met Kim. It was shortly after Christopher had signed his record deal with Bad Boy. She was sitting at the kitchen table when I came home. I pulled Christopher to the side.

"Who is that little girl?" I asked him.

"Ma, that ain't no little girl. That's a grown woman and she's one of my artists. Her name is Lil' Kim and she's part of Junior M.A.F.I.A."

I didn't see her much after that. The next time I saw her was onstage.

I was at the hairdresser one day. I had been going to this hairdresser for quite some time, so they knew me and they knew of my son. She knew that while I was proud of Christopher and supported his career, I didn't talk about him or his famous friends.

"Ms. Wallace, I don't know if you know Kim personally," she started reluctantly. "But perhaps you will get to see her. And if you do, would you please tell her to shave her pubic hair."

What!

My hairdresser said that she had attended a concert at Radio City Music Hall and Kim was performing.

"She really needs to groom herself," she said. "It was disgusting."

I imagined everyone in the shop was listening and could hear everything that she said. I was grateful that my chair wasn't facing anyone so I wouldn't have to look at their faces, because I certainly wanted to hide mine. After all, this was my son's artist. And whatever Christopher did somehow always came back to me. I felt embarrassed.

I decided to go to this show myself. Kim was performing at Radio City. I would try to attend anything that involved Christopher—especially if it took place in New York.

So I decided to go to Radio City Music Hall to see the Bad Boy Tour. I imagined that my hairdresser was exaggerating. And I didn't want to go into the performance with any preconceived notions. I don't remember exactly where I was sitting, but I was close to the stage. I remember having nervous energy because this was a really big night for Bad Boy. I found myself looking around at all the faces, hoping they enjoyed the show. I kept thinking about what my hairdresser had told me, and I just hoped that when Kim stepped onstage that night, nothing at all in her pubic area would be showing.

Kim was the opening act and I knew it was going to be a long night. The curtain opened to a spotlight shining on a bed. Kim rolled out of that bed and walked to the edge of the stage, and everything my hairdresser had talked about was staring me right in the face. She was rapping into the microphone, but another pair of lips were moving. She opened her legs as wide as she could at the front of the stage, and I saw every vaginal fold that she could possibly have.

She had on what I think was a little skirt. Without it, she would have been naked. I thought the least she could have done was wear a thong. It was the most disgusting thing I had ever seen with my own eyes. Needless to say, that was the last time I saw Kim perform. But it wouldn't be the last time I dealt with her.

■ ■ ■

I decided to leave Brooklyn and move to my son's home in New Jersey and maintain an office in Brooklyn. Faith and I decided to get rid of a lot of Christopher's business baggage. I simply could not trust some of his old associates. Bad Boy was concerned with its self-interests and not ours.

Faith and I hired our own lawyers and accountant and started from scratch with a team that we handpicked to help me manage Christopher's estate. While it seemed that I had one part of my new life heading in the right direction, I was blindsided by the nasty way my son's name was being dragged through the media.

Once the negative media coverage started, all I could think about were my grandchildren. These lies would not be what Christopher's children would have to remember him by. I had to make sure that my son's

friendship

legacy outlived and outweighed whatever they wrote about him, whatever they said about him—for the sake of my grandchildren.

I'm the only one who can truly tell them who their father was. He was not a murderous, drug-dealing monster. He was a man with a tremendous love for his children, family, and friends. He was a young man with a dream that he worked extremely hard to make come true. He was gifted with words and could tell a story like no other individual. My son simply made a living by making profound statements in his music.

To this day, Christopher is one of the most loyal human beings I have ever known. And it was a sentiment he expected in others. But he learned the hard way that this was not always the case. The truth is, Christopher accepted the illusion of a friend and mentor for about $25,000. That's the amount Puffy lured my son with.

That was a lot of money for Christopher back then as a nineteen-year-old. He had never seen that much at one time in his life. I imagine it was a lot of money for any young person—black or white, male or female—growing up in urban America. It was enough money to make my son believe that Puffy was ready to do anything for him. It was enough to buy a blind love and loyalty. That same admiration and loyalty have that young rapper that many have compared to my son—Shyne—in jail with a ten-year sentence. I believe Sean loved my son—after he was dead.

I didn't run the streets with my son so I can only rely on the twenty-four years that I knew him and how he was with me. Loyalty was a big

loyalty and trust

thing with him, to a fault. I used to tell Christopher all the time not to trust Sean, but he wouldn't hear any of that. I told Christopher that he needed to become more knowledgeable about the business side of his career. But Christopher, with his extremely loyal self, couldn't take me talking about Sean even when I had my son's best interests at heart.

"Ma, chill!" he would say. "You can't be talking about my man like that."

He eventually got to see what I was talking about, though, firsthand. He found out that he was grossly underpaid for his publishing rights. I opened my mouth to say, "I told you so." But Christopher stopped me in my tracks, knowing what was coming:

"Stop talking about him, Ma. That's enough! I don't care what he did because he makes it happen. All I know is that this kid is a

his friends

millionaire and he said he is going to make me one, too. And that needs to happen."

It made me even angrier to see that Christopher would accept being undercut by a friend. But you know what? It didn't matter what I thought about Puffy because Christopher had already made up his mind. Puffy was his friend and that was that. Even if he wasn't Christopher's friend, Christopher was going to hold up his end of the friendship until the very end. It was something I couldn't argue with. It was admirable.

I know that Christopher was far from perfect. But I do know one thing: he was a good man at his core.

I know he made some mistakes—many I don't even know about. And most of his mistakes were because he was too trusting and because he wasn't as worldly as people made him out to be. My son was part of a high-stakes game and didn't know the rules.

I'm glad that my son does not have to witness that the very people that he thought he could ride and die with wouldn't think twice about using his mother. I'm glad he doesn't have to know that they wouldn't think twice about exploiting his children. I am glad that he's not here to see how they have used his image and his name.

I was in my Brooklyn office one morning planning the earliest stages of Christopher's charity—the Christopher Wallace Foundation. I got a call that seemed to be out of the blue. Kim's assistant asked if Kim could do an interview at my home in New Jersey. She explained that Kim was living

with her mother and that their home was not appropriate for an inter-view—especially for someone who was supposed to be a rap star with a lot of money.

It was just one more thing about the business that disturbed my spirit. The lives that these artists portrayed were lies—for many of them. And these lies trickled down to the inner city, making young people aspire to live the life they saw these so-called rap stars living with $100,000 cars, $50,000 watches, and million-dollar homes. But these were all lies. They set these young people up to chase a big fat lie. And the select few who did have the "things" paid a price to get there.

But aside from the lie Kim was living, I didn't think anything was wrong with her coming to my home and conducting an interview. I wanted to embrace the people my son considered his friends. And I did what I could for them. I made provisions for Kim to use the home in Bergen County, New Jersey, while I was out working.

I imagined a simple interview being conducted in my living room. That couldn't have been any further from reality. About two months later, someone came up to me and said, "Oh, Miss Wallace, did you check out this magazine? There are some really nice pictures inside, and did you see Kim's picture?" She pulls out the magazine and shows me.

The first picture I saw was Kim wearing my son's mink coat, holding his chain, and wearing his hat. I was in shock. I felt violated. This was such an invasion of my privacy. Those things were in personal areas of my home. She had had to rummage through my stuff to wear the things she did.

When I got home, I called Kim's people who'd set up the photo shoot. They gave me a few apologies, saying that they didn't think it meant anything.

"You didn't think it meant anything to me!" I said.

I hung up, disgusted. I read the entire article and learned that not only was Kim wearing things belonging to my son, but she claimed that the home belonged to her as well. This experience helped me draw my own opinions about Kim. And they weren't good.

As much as I tried to distance myself from Kim, the more she seemed to be around. Radio disc jockeys Ed Lover and Dr. Dre, who were hosting a morning show on HOT-97 at the time, were pretty popular around the time of my son's death. I had the radio on one morning and heard them talking about me.

"What's going on in the Wallace household?" Ed said. Then he talked about a supposed feud among me, Faith, and Lil' Kim. They were saying that we were all fighting over Biggie's ashes.

"I hear Kim has the ashes," Dr. Dre said.

"No, I hear Faith has the ashes," Ed says. "Miss Wallace, what's going on?"

I picked up the phone and called in and told them that none of what they were saying was true.

"You're just putting out more nasty lies to the public!" I said.

But that was just the beginning of more lies and deception and disappointment.

beginning
of deception

FRIEND OF MINE?

turn back the hands of time...

"Wish I could turn back the hands of time..." Those are words spoken by Puffy in the song "I'll Be Missing You," which he dedicated to my son. I wish he could turn back the hands of time. I wish he could bring Christopher back. I wonder if things would be different.

Years after Christopher's death I found myself still looking for the friends who claimed to have loved my son—those who pledged their loyalty and undying friendship. Where are they now?

Lil' Cease was another one of my son's "best friends." He used to hang around the house often. He was there early in Christopher's career. And my son truly loved that young man. He would often tell me, "Ma, that's my man, my protégé." I believed that.

After my son died, I would have done anything for Lil' Cease, as close as he was to Christopher. My son felt so genuinely for him that I also loved Cease. I loved him so much that when he didn't have a place to live, I welcomed him into my home. When he moved out and finally got himself together, do you think he kept in contact with me? Not until he needed something again. Years passed and I could count the number of times that he called.

I did finally get a call from Cease—from jail. He had been arrested on a gun charge. He called me to bail him out. And I didn't hesitate. I did it because he and his mother reached out to me and I know that Christopher would have done it if he were alive.

When Cease was fresh out of his jail cell, he thanked me and told me how much he appreciated me bailing him out. Months—and I mean several months later—he called me and told me that the case was over. I was under the impression that the case had been thrown out or settled, and he didn't volunteer any details on exactly what had happened with the gun and why he'd been arrested, so I decided not to ask.

I assumed with everything being over, I had nothing to do except wait to get my money back. But the money never came. I called my lawyer and asked him to check into Cease's case.

My attorney researched it and gave it to me straight: "Miss Wallace, you've been lied to."

He told me that Cease's case was far from being settled and he still needed to go back to court. I called Wayne, one of Christopher's managers. (Mark was his other manager. Mark mostly worked out of his office, while Wayne would do the actual footwork with Christopher.) Wayne would often come to my house to pick up Christopher for appearances or any other business. I spoke with Wayne quite a bit before and after Christopher's death.

Wayne is a wonderful person. The thing I liked most about him was that his personality was consistent. Every time I saw him, he had a smile on his face. After Christopher passed away, Wayne and I got even closer. We started to develop a mother-son bond. I had so many questions after Christopher's death, and he was so patient with me. He never once talked down to me. Wayne would really listen to everything that I was saying and asking and showed me a lot of respect.

So I called Wayne and explained everything to him. He'd never known that I was the one who'd bailed Cease out. I told him that nine months had passed and I still hadn't gotten my bail money back. Wayne was shocked and furious. He went to the courthouse himself, got the papers, and sent them to me via FedEx. Then he paid a visit to the bail bondsman. Two weeks later, I got my money back.

Cease only needed to have one piece of paper signed by his lawyer for my money to be returned. He could not bother to do that. He didn't care, not as long as he'd got what he wanted and needed from me. It was hurtful to think that he didn't have the respect or heart to make sure his "best friend's" mother got her money back. Once again, I had seen the real side of someone whom my son had held dear to his heart.

respect

The real kicker and probably one of the most disloyal things was what I heard one afternoon. I was in the car in New York taking care of some business, and the radio was tuned to 107.5 WBLS and the *Wendy Williams Experience*. Cease was on talking about a bad contract that he was bound to with Kim and all the drama surrounding that. He also discussed that he'd gone to jail. At the end of the interview he had the audacity to give a shout-out to Jay-Z and thank him for bailing him out of jail when he'd got arrested.

It was a blessing that I don't drive because I would certainly have driven into a hydrant or onto the curb. I was numb and in serious shock. It was me, Voletta Wallace, on behalf of my son, Christopher Wallace, who'd bailed out Lil' Cease—my son's so-called best friend. Cease was the one Christopher wanted to succeed in the business more than anyone else.

It was me, Voletta Wallace, who waited for almost a year to get my money back. I was the one who'd had to hire a lawyer and wait to have $250,000 in bail money returned to me. I guess in a business of lies and deception it just sounded better for him to say it was Jay-Z who'd bailed him out. Perhaps the whole lie put him in good standing with Jay-Z. I'm sure he said it in the hope of getting something out of it. Lil' Cease and Lil' Kim are both one and the same. They deserve each other.

I often hear my son's work on the radio and on television, and it always feels good. I'm so proud that he left his mark on the world. And somehow it feels as if I'm in his presence when one of his songs comes on the radio out of nowhere. It's a blessing for me to see and hear my son long after his passing. But sometimes it's bittersweet. It has become a full-time job for me to try to stop the media and greedy people from distorting my son's memory.

bitter-sweet

Lil' Kim was clearly haunting me. Her album was about to drop that week, and it seemed whenever the television was on, there she was. In every interview, it seemed to me, that she was never talking about herself. Every other breath was about my son. If she wasn't blaming him for forcing her to get an abortion, she was saying that he beat her and that she was not wearing glasses to be fashionable but because of a scar left near her eye and bruises left on her by my son.

Every time I heard her speak she had something new and more salacious to say about my son.

I was furious and I was furious for his children. What kind of monster was she making my son out to be? Here he was this big man allegedly beating up a woman who didn't weigh a hundred pounds. She had me questioning my son. She had me asking, "Christopher, did you really do these things?"

If he really did and I were Kim, I would have hated him and turned him in to the authorities. I met up with one of her friends, and I use that term *friend* loosely because friendship and love seem to take on a different meaning in the world of hip-hop.

"Please tell Kim to just come out and say every horrible thing my son ever did to her so I can stop being shocked," I told her friend.

I wish Kim had said these things while he was alive so that he could have defended himself. It's cruel to wait until someone is silenced to make these kinds of allegations. Two weeks later she was on a radio show, and there she was talking again about my son, and it amazed me how she would go from my son being a monster to her, to being her mentor.

I realized that she had an album coming out and all the bullshit she was saying was solely for publicity. I don't think she cared who got hurt. I guess sympathy will sell a few more albums.

I resent Kim like no other for trying to build her wealth and happiness on someone else's tragedy.

I decided that I needed to put my anger to better use and focus my energies on the Christopher Wallace Foundation. I wanted to do something that would make my son proud. The foundation sends books into

the hip hop world

inner-city schools—particularly in our old Brooklyn neighborhood—and provides summer outlets for young people. We hold basketball tournaments and we take the kids on various trips throughout the summer to places like Six Flags Great Adventure.

In 2003, I decided to make the Christopher Wallace Foundation even bigger. I invited the parents of anyone who'd lost a child in the entertainment business—mothers of Tupac Shakur, Big Pun, Freaky Tah, etc. The event was promoted as BIG Night Out and was capped off by a black-tie dinner.

I made the rounds to the popular New York radio stations, including the controversial *Wendy Williams Experience* on WBLS. Faith accompanied me to this interview. Wendy Williams is known in New York City for her outrageous interviews. She usually focuses on scandal and gossip. I was happy to go on her show because I knew I would be reaching a lot of people—she has a huge audience. And these people were some of my son's biggest fans.

Faith came with me for support because Wendy is known to be a tough interviewer. And true to form, she asked me some of the most provocative questions about my son and Kim.

Kim had apparently alleged that Christopher had abused her and held a gun to her head. I was so angry and frustrated and fed up with these claims that I lost it. When Wendy asked me about the gun, I just blurted out, "If it's true, if in fact Christopher did hold a gun to her head, he should have pulled the trigger and blown her brains out!"

The statement silenced the entire studio. In that moment, if I could have scooped up every word and shoved them back into my mouth, I would have. I was immediately sorry I'd said it. And I had to ask myself, did I mean it? Absolutely not. I was angry and frustrated that I had to defend my son's name against someone who I believe is a liar.

I'm sorry that I ever met Kim. And I'm sorry that my granddaughter met her. Kim's an embarrassment and promotes the most vile stereotypes of women. She has no limits to what she would do for money, and that's a sad place to be.

I went shopping one day with my granddaughter. We were in Times Square in midtown Manhattan. As we were heading toward Forty-second Street, my granddaughter screamed at the top of her lungs, "Me-ma, look at Kim! Ooh! Me-ma! Her tookie is out."

It was a giant billboard near the MTV building of Kim squatting in a suggestive pose. It's a shame that as an artist she hasn't changed or grown a single bit. She's still trying to sell sex, and she's sinking lower and lower with every attempt. It's my hope that one day she becomes a real woman.

Even with all that I feel and believe about Kim, I would never want to see any harm come to her. And I would certainly not want to see her brains blown out. I wish I could take that one statement back.

I now know that while a lot of tears were shed for the true love and loss of my son, just as many tears were shed because he was the money train that so many rode. Christopher's death hit a lot of his "friends" where it really hurt—their pockets. They mourned that their money train had stopped moving, not so much that they had lost a special person.

lost a
special
person

BIGGIE & TUPAC:
FRIEND OR FOE?

what are these wings on my back?

"Bad Boys move in silence. If someone wants to get your ass, they're gonna wake up in heaven. There ain't no record gonna be made about it ... it's gonna be straight up. 'Oh, shit, where am I? What are these, wings on my back?'"

Sean Combs made this statement in a *Vibe* magazine interview shortly after the death of Tupac. It added more fuel to the fire that perhaps Sean and the Bad Boy crew had had something to do with the murder of Tupac.

The murderer of Tupac has still not been found. Neither has the murderer of my son. And while I do not know for sure that Puffy had nothing to do with Tupac's death, I know for a fact that my son did not. Both he and Tupac, I believe, were pawns in an intricate chess game played by two thugs. Tupac and Christopher were the talent, they were the moneymakers. They had more talent in their pinkie nails than Puffy and Suge Knight have in their entire bodies put together. Manipulation is not talent.

The truth is that Christopher and Tupac were close friends of music. Tupac used to call the house for Christopher all the time. From what I understand, they were buddies, helping each other attain success in the rap business. I could envision them doing records together and building an empire together. Their talent together, can you imagine?

That dream was shattered on November 30, 1994. That was the night that Tupac was shot five times—including two shots that grazed his head. He was on his way to the Quad Recording Studios in Manhattan where he was going to record his third solo album, *Me Against the World*. He was shot in the lobby of the studio and robbed of $40,000 in jewelry.

Christopher and Sean were at the same studio upstairs at the time of the shooting. Somehow they were implicated. While police ruled out any involvement, Tupac and his camp would not buy it. I believe the implication of my son in that shooting was instigated by outside parties who could benefit from Tupac being enemies with Christopher rather than friends.

Tupac was to later say that he felt his shooting was an ambush, a setup, and he named Christopher as a culprit. I believe it was a setup. It was set up to look as if Christopher had something to do with it.

east coast

Unfortunately, we may never know the truth. The truth I know is that Christopher had nothing to do with it.

Between outside forces and the media, hell-bent on creating some sort of East Coast–West Coast feud, some sort of rap wars, these young men didn't have a chance. I could relate to this years later after Christopher was murdered when the media had me and Faith at odds, fighting in a California hotel over what to do with Christopher's body. The truth then was that we could not have supported one another more; we could not have been closer at that time. So I know how easily truth can be distorted and how people will capitalize on those lies for their own purposes.

After Tupac was shot in New York, Christopher was distraught. We talked for hours about it. I remember asking him, "Christopher, why did Tupac fight for that jewelry? Why didn't he just give those crooks whatever they wanted?"

"Ma, think about it," Christopher said. "You work so hard for everything; you're not just going to give it up. You're going to fight back. I don't blame him for fighting back; I'm just sorry that he had to get shot like that."

Christopher was one of the first people to visit Tupac in the hospital. And Christopher hated hospitals, but he had to go and let Tupac know that he was there for him. I know he told Tupac, "If there is anything I can do for you, just let me know." They were still friends then. They were still buddies. But with the help of comments made by both Puffy and Suge Knight, it turned. I'm just sad that it turned so easily. I'm sad that Tupac

vs. WEST COAST feud

could be swayed to think that my son was capable of betraying him. I know that hurt Christopher deeply.

Then it started getting nasty. Not only was Tupac making statements about Christopher and how he had had something to do with the shooting or at the very least knew who did, but he also started taking his anger out in his music and even involved Faith. He was calling Christopher out every chance he got. I remember seeing him on television jumping around, gesticulating, saying, "Yeah, Biggie, come see me," and, "Biggie, let's talk." It sounded threatening. He was behaving like Christopher's number-one enemy. I couldn't believe that this was the same young man who would call my house and say, "Hi, Ma! Is Biggie there?"

I couldn't believe it. *My God, how did it get this far?*

In the midst of the controversy, it seemed that Christopher's career was growing even bigger. My son was up and coming faster than anyone else in the rap world. He, for the first time that I recall, actually was serious about something. He had a vision for himself with his music career. He was not looking to be involved with any rivalry.

He had a mantra: negativity brings failure and I'm not trying to fail at this. That's where Christopher's head was. He wasn't interested in being in the middle of a feud or a rap war. He wanted to be successful. My son had something to live for. He had the love of his family—he had me, he had Faith, he had T'yanna, and he had CJ. He had the love of his fans.

negativity brings failure

He was even making dreams come true for so many of the young people who'd grown up in the neighborhood. He had formed a group—Junior M.A.F.I.A.—that was also getting some attention, with Lil' Cease and Lil' Kim breaking out. Christopher had big, big dreams. He had a plan. He had a grand vision.

On the other side of the world was Suge Knight. He, too, had a vision. But he was a different type of animal altogether. He had money and power but he didn't seem to want peace. He didn't seem happy with happiness. For some reason, he chose to attach his soul to the most violent and vile things on the street.

Suge Knight is darkness, to me. And where there is no light, nothing can grow and nothing can prosper. If you allow him to pull you into his grip, it is only a matter of time before you will be gone, and that can happen in two ways. Either you will remove yourself from his presence while you are alive, or you will end up dead.

Now, I'm no prophet on this matter. The evidence is all around him. He hooked up with Dr. Dre, and Dr. Dre had to go. Dre has since gone on to find tremendous success as the mastermind behind sensation Eminem.

Snoop Doggy Dogg was with Suge. And when a window of opportunity opened a crack after Suge went to jail, Snoop climbed through and didn't look back. He, too, has gone on to find tremendous success, not only in music, but also in the movies. Tupac was not so lucky.

On September 7, 1996, Tupac was gunned down on a Las Vegas street while in the passenger seat of a car driven by Suge Knight. He had spent that evening with Suge at a Mike Tyson fight. Ironically, Tupac used to wear a bulletproof vest, but was allegedly asked to take it off because it was illegal to wear one in the MGM Grand Hotel where the fight took place.

Christopher was in the hospital when Tupac was murdered. I broke the news to him. He was recovering from a broken leg suffered in a car accident on the New Jersey Turnpike.

When I walked into the hospital room, I said, "Christopher, did you see the news? Did you hear that Tupac passed away?"

He didn't believe me when I told him. He insisted that I hadn't heard all of the news about the shooting.

"Ma, trust me, Pac is not dead," Christopher said. "I know Duke and he is going to bounce back."

Tupac did seem invincible. He was shot five times and survived. This time it seemed as if he would pull through again. He lived for six days after the shooting.

"I don't know, Ma," Christopher said. "Maybe they're saying all that for publicity. I know Duke is going to bounce back. Pac has been shot so many times that I know he's still living. I can't believe he's dead."

Tupac was definitely dead. But I couldn't convince Christopher. He was in denial. I knew he would eventually know the truth. So I continued

cherish life

our visit and we changed the subject. When Christopher got out of the hospital, he reconciled with Tupac's indeed being dead, which hit him pretty hard.

Christopher didn't have long to mourn before he, too, was a victim—less than a year later. He and Tupac will now forever be linked—two young men cut down in their prime with promising careers, millions of fans, loving mothers.

Tupac's mother, Afeni, and I have also been bound together. Our relationship was born out of the tragedies we have both suffered. While we aren't best friends, we are women who understand what we've been through and share an experience that few people have shared. We call each other from time to time to touch base, and we talk when a situation arises where either of us needs to talk. I know every pain is different, but I know every day she feels the pain of losing her son, because I do.

People often assume that I'm depressed on May 21, Christopher's birthday. But that's not the case. I raised Christopher to cherish life and to cherish every single day. So I spend that day celebrating his life, not moping around depressed over his death. I was able to rely on God and my faith to get me through the tough times without dwelling too much on the pain.

Christopher had a conscience and was raised as a Christian. He went to church every Sunday until he was fourteen years old, then he decided to stop going. He told me that he would go back one day, but for now "God understands."

For twenty-one years I have been searching for the truth—I studied the Bible for years. I also decided to leave our Baptist church around the same time Christopher did. I was in search of answers and had a lot of unanswered questions—so I became a Jehovah's Witness.

I remember when I told Christopher I was going to become a Jehovah's Witness. The first thing he said was "So, you mean I'm not going to have any more birthdays?"

"You're going to have a birthday every day," I said.

"Well, what about Christmas? Because I know they don't celebrate that."

"Christopher, first of all, Christmas is just in people's minds. It's the art of giving. They are not celebrating a birthday that happened more than two thousand years ago. So if it's just about giving gifts, you get gifts all the time."

"Yeah, yeah, that's true. So what about the birthday part? Tell me about that again."

"Every day is your birthday. It's just like Mother's Day. I'm not expecting you to give me a gift on Mother's Day. I don't think there should be a designated day for mothers because I'm your mother every day. I'm not waiting for a gift from you on Valentine's Day. You love me every day, right?"

"Okay, I'm cool with that. There is only one thing that I'm not cool with and that's you going around and knocking on people's doors and people being nasty to you, because I don't want to have to hurt nobody."

"Don't worry about it. I go out with friends, and if they insult me, I can take it. If I have something to share and they don't want to accept it, they can say, 'No, thank you.' But if they are nasty, then they are the losers."

So Christopher accepted my religion and accepted that every day was special, and if he gave me a gift, I had better not ask what it was for because he would say, "Oh, it's just Mother's Day."

I think the one thing that I am most proud of about Christopher was his heart condition. He was a giver to anyone who asked. He was a man of his word. And he was loyal. All of these things are conditions of the heart that I know I helped to develop and instill in him.

I'm blessed with the opportunity to instill those same values in his children. But unfortunately his daughter is growing up in a difficult situation because she understands so much of what is said about her father. Furthermore, T'yanna is being raised by a woman who has chosen not to expound or make clear her life and create her own sense of achievement (if for no other reason than that her daughter, T'yanna, is watching). T'yanna lost a father to whom she was close, and I have to watch her mother live off of my son's resources. She is living in a typical world of materialism and shallowness.

I have never approved of Rose because even when she and my son were dating, even before T'yanna, I saw her for what she is. I didn't see a woman with any goals, any aspirations, or a plan for her life.

man of his word

However, I pray constantly that she will turn herself around and live to improve herself rather than live off some inheritance that doesn't even belong to her. While I do all that I can for T'yanna, I know that it is Rose who will ultimately have the biggest impact on my granddaughter. She is her mother and she is the one with her day to day.

I now live in a quiet community outside of New York, and it has a great school system. At all cost I want my granddaughter to have the best of everything, so I called Rose and asked if she wanted a home so that T'yanna could go to school in this new town. She said yes.

With funds from Christopher's estate, Faith and I were pleased to purchase a beautiful home for Rose to raise my granddaughter. While I hoped the home would motivate her to want more and do more with her life, as of today, it hasn't. It bothers me because I know that if I see it, T'yanna sees it. I have never known her to ever hold a job or attend school to work toward a degree. I have a great deal of respect for Rose, but she resents my interfering. My heart aches that she doesn't feel the need to set an example for her daughter.

I believe that children need to see their parents going through the struggle, working hard, and making it happen. Children need to see their parents clean the house and make a home for them. Parents must set a standard. I did that for Christopher, and I believe a great deal of his success can be attributed to the foundation that I set for him.

I know he would be upset to see how Rose is raising his daughter, and if he were alive, it wouldn't be that way. I don't say much to Rose because I don't feel I have a right. She has shown me that the relationship between us is strictly financial.

T'yanna may decide because of what she sees from her mother that when she grows up, she's not going to do anything because she has financial resources waiting for her. I know that whatever amount of money she inherits, if she has that attitude, it will burn away.

Whenever I have the opportunity to spend time with T'yanna, I sit her down and talk to her about life. I tell her things that I don't think her mother tells her. I make sure to teach her right from wrong.

And after she processes this, I am certain that T'yanna will make the right choices. I am confident that she will have her own mind, but I want her heart conditioned to know right from wrong. I pray for her to live a clean life so that she can distinguish negative paths from the positive ones. I'm not necessarily hoping for her to be a nuclear physicist or a doctor. If she becomes a garbage collector, I would not mind that at all as long as she is living a decent, clean life. If she becomes a nurse, that would be wonderful, but her heart needs to be in the right place and she needs to take her own path. And the same goes for CJ.

about life

Faith has been quite another story when it comes to raising children. She is a hardworking young woman who loves and cares for her children and shows it in more ways than one. I see it not only in the way she treats her children but also in the way her children behave. It's not fake. She is genuine.

Showing love isn't buying your child an expensive pet or toy. Showing love is being strict when you have to be and doling out hugs and kisses in between. And more important—if you want your children to grow up with morals and values and a strong sense of purpose, you have to show them those qualities. You can't party, drink, smoke, and curse and tell your children that those things are bad. If you want them to be successful, you have to show them success in your actions and your character. If your child doesn't see that from you, from whom and where is he or she going to learn it?

My son never saw another man in our home. He never had to deal with "Oh, that's my mother's man" or "She has a new boyfriend." He never saw me locked in a room with a man inside. I don't believe women should bring men around their children unless they are marrying them. If you cannot bring a man to your child and say, "This is going to be your stepfather," I believe you should keep that man away. I cannot stand seeing children who have a new "uncle" every other month.

My son never saw that from me. And my grandchildren will never see it. The only time I'm locked in a room is to be with them, reading them a story or playing. That is the life I led with my son, and that is the life I continue to lead because that's what I'm about. I am proud of the way I raised my son, and I am happy with how I am having a positive impact on my son's children.

The worst thing that you can have as a parent is regrets. Once you're gone, whatever you have put into your child is final. Actually it happens before that. If you don't get the good stuff in early, you can lose your child forever.

If you are like me and have the misfortune to see your child die before you and bury your child, then you have to know in your heart that you did everything humanly possible to make sure your child was on his or her

morals and values

way to being the best person he or she could have been, and that you never missed an opportunity to be all the mother or all the father you could have been.

You cannot plan or predict life but so much. I planned to have been dead about seven years ago. Instead, I buried my son.

I am
proud
of the way
I raised
my son

MY LIFE
AFTER DEATH

Is there life after death?

My entire life has been an incredible journey. It started with my receiving a one-in-a-million-chance plane ticket to visit the country that I had dreamed about my entire life, then led to my being something I'd never imagined— a single mother in Brooklyn. Then to living out the impossible—seeing my only child reach a level of success that few ever get to see. And through all of that, I battled breast cancer, which I beat, but before I could fully enjoy my victory over death, I had to bury my son— a victim of a murder that is still unsolved.

Not once did I ever ask, "Why me!" I know that bad things happen to good people. And if I were to question the bad things that happened to me, then I must also question the good.

When I was sick or when I found myself burdened with problems, I also never considered that as my faith being tested. I looked at it as the devil trying to tempt me, not God testing me. And I was determined not to let the devil get the best of me. Bad things happen, but I know God did not allow them to happen. I know the devil wants me to feel bad, angry, distraught, and desperate. So I continued to push forward and I continued to do what I felt was right.

For me, the right thing has been charity, giving back. I have always been a hard worker. Even when Christopher was making a lot of money, I never considered not working. I needed to work. After his death and after leaving teaching, I decided to change my focus and find something new to work hard at. I decided to start a foundation in Christopher's name. It was an exciting prospect—the possibility of bringing hope to thousands of young people. It would be an extension of what I had brought to my classes for so many years.

I would focus on readings and books because I have always believed that reading is the key to unlocking success. Through books, even children locked away in poverty in a Brooklyn neighborhood can travel to wonderful places and open the windows of their minds to what the world

reading is the key to success

has to offer. The foundation would bring books to children in inner-city neighborhoods and also provide them with camping experiences to show them trees and grass and water—to show them a world beyond their urban neighborhood.

In March 2003, I put everything I had into The B.I.G. Night Out Christopher Memorial Foundation. I hired a staff of wonderful people who also put their hearts into the event, and we pulled it off with record success. It was the black-tie event of the year for the hip-hop community. I prayed beforehand that it would go perfectly, but the night was even bigger and better than I could ever have imagined.

hip-hop community

The energy from B.I.G. Night Out stayed with me for days after it was over. And while I was feeling well physically, I was scheduled for a checkup, which I got regularly, especially since my breast cancer scare. I had my regular physical as well as a mammography, which every woman over the age of fifty should have every year. It was all pretty routine.

However, after my examination, the doctor suggested I get a sonogram. Something on the mammogram concerned him. After the sonogram, I got a call from my doctor to contact my surgeon because a biopsy was needed. *Here we go again!*

Several days later, the biopsy results were in: breast cancer. It had reared its ugly head back into my life.

What have I done wrong this time? I thought. I watched my diet. I was extra careful with my health. I was living as stress-free as I could. But none of that mattered.

The doctor who had seen me through my first bout with breast cancer had retired. I would have given anything to have him back as my doctor. At least I would have felt comfortable about going through this process again instead of having to start over with someone new, and perhaps someone not as qualified.

So here I am, round two in my battle with cancer, with a brand-new doctor. The nurse told me that before anything was official, I would undergo a few procedures in the doctor's office. But I was not comfortable with this new doctor and did not want him to do a thing to my body. I told the receptionist who was responsible for making my appointment with the doctor that I wanted someone else.

"Oh, I know who I'm going to recommend to you," the receptionist said. "Dr. Carroll."

I didn't know Dr. Carroll from Dr. Eve, I was just happy to have a female doctor. On the day of the appointment I arrived at the clinic and walked up to the nurses' station, signed my name, and told them I was there to see "Dr. Carroll."

I'm not sure why I had to wait so long, but it was more than I could tolerate at that point, so I went back up to the nurses' station and said, "Is she in today?" The assistant turned and looked at me so strangely. She said, "Dr. Carroll is not a she. Dr. Carroll is a *he*."

I was so angry I wanted to hit someone. That my new doctor was going to be a woman had been the last bit of comfort I'd had to hold on to. But I could do nothing at that point. It was out of my hands. I was so mad I think fire was coming out of my ears.

The nurse escorted me to an examining room and in comes this bouncy child person. It was Dr. Carroll. My attitude changed almost immediately. He was one of the most pleasant people I had ever met. All I could see the moment he walked in were his teeth.

He ordered me to have another sonogram. When the results of the sonogram came back, he scheduled me for an in-office biopsy. The thought of having another biopsy just scared me to the core. I remembered how much the first one had hurt.

Dr. Carroll did the biopsy and held my hand tightly. I was shaking so badly that I couldn't control it. He looked me right in the eye and told me to trust him that it was not going to hurt. I swear with all of me that he looked me dead in the eyes and did all that he needed to do so that I felt no pain. I don't know if he hypnotized me, but it did not hurt.

"See, I told you," he said with a smile.

After the procedure was over, he told me that nothing came out that was useful, so I would need to check into the hospital for another procedure—one that would require surgery. On the day of my appointment, it snowed really badly and I could not get there from the countryside. So we rescheduled the appointment for another day. Two of my friends came with me the following week.

After the procedure, my surgeon did not hesitate to tell me that I would need a mastectomy. I had had a mastectomy on my right breast during my first bout with cancer. This time, I was taking it hard. This new cancer scare seemed to come out of left field, and I was not at all prepared mentally for what I was about to go through. I was mad, I was so furious. I don't know whom I was furious with, but I just was.

I was scheduled to have the surgery at a hospital that I did not care for, but my doctor told me if he did the surgery at my hospital, his personal staff could not be there. He said that if I didn't do it at his hospital, I would not have the benefit of seeing him frequently after the surgery. I figured if I was going to work with him, it had to be with his staff, so I decided to go to his hospital.

mentally prepared

Before I actually went into the hospital for my surgery, one of the hardest things in addition to facing my own mortality again was telling my granddaughter. When I told her I had to go into the hospital, she said, "I don't want you to go to the hospital." I told her that I had to. She had the most worried look on her face.

"I will make sure that someone calls you the minute I am out of surgery," I assured her.

"Me-ma, I don't want you to go to the hospital" was all she kept saying.

Her maternal grandmother had gone into the hospital a couple of years before this and never came out. And she didn't want to experience that again. T'yanna was with me the day her maternal grandmother died and she said, "Grandma should never have gone into the hospital. If she had stayed home, she wouldn't have died."

I made sure to spend as much time as possible with T'yanna before I went in. I made sure to talk to her about the procedure I was going to have. I told her about my first mastectomy and how I was still here to be with her. And I told her that I was going to the hospital because the doctor had found cancer in my other breast. And as I held her little body, I let her know that I would do everything in my power to make sure I would return home to give her hugs and kisses again. And I meant it.

The surgery was hell—again. When I came to after the anesthesia, another part of my body was now gone. The pain was excruciating. But I managed to get in a question after I got out of surgery:

"How did it go?"

Dr. Carroll said that it looked good and that I might not have to go through chemotherapy. He scheduled an appointment for me with the oncologist for the following week. The results from that visit would determine if I would, in fact, be able to skip chemotherapy. Chemotherapy is one of the worst experiences you can imagine. Chemotherapy kills microscopic disease that may still be hanging around after they've removed the tumor. You take it to attack the disease that cannot be seen by a scan. It travels along the blood lines.

When my test came back, Dr. Carroll informed me that I would be doing the chemo. He said that they treat cancer more aggressively now. Ten years ago they could have given me chemo the first time, too. But today, they take no chances. The good thing was that I didn't have to have more than six or eight treatments. Everyone was optimistic that I would pull through like a champ. Dr. Carroll told me about the side effects, such as nausea and losing my hair, something I was not looking forward to at all. But I'm glad he prepared me so that I wouldn't be shocked when clumps of my hair started coming out in the shower.

Two months prior to my surgery, I had cut my hair. So I was in the hospital with short hair and I had just taken my braids out. One week later after the chemo, I was in the shower and washing my hair and I felt the silky strands in my fingers. I just looked at my hands and said, "Oh my God! The time has come."

Then I took a comb and I combed my hair back and all of it was in the comb. I said to myself, "Okay, this it." There were other side effects that my doctor hadn't mentioned. Shortly after my hair fell out, I started having pains in my left leg and trouble walking. It hurt so bad that I needed a cane to walk. The oncologist told me that when the chemo was over, I would be able to get back to my life. But it was a long time before that actually happened.

One of the things that got me through this latest battle with cancer was having my granddaughter, T'yanna, close to me. Her presence has been a real comfort to me. Having her around gives me hope and something to live for. She has been a little trouper for me.

Life has not stopped for me, it has just slowed down. My next goal is to put out my son's next album and make sure it represents him in a special way. And after the album, I will pour my energies into the next Christopher Wallace Memorial Foundation event. I want to continue to put books in schools.

I am also planning to get involved with even more causes that will give something back to humanity. Dr. Carroll goes to Haiti once a year for a week and donates his time treating the underprivileged on that impoverished and destitute island. He performs radical mastectomies on women and has been doing so without a functioning mammogram machine. We don't know how fortunate we are here in America. I will be helping him get a mammogram machine for the hospital in Haiti. I'm looking forward

to providing some help for women going through the same thing I went through.

I have found that giving of my time and energy has been the biggest source of comfort and healing for me during the most difficult times in my life.

I often find myself wondering if I had to live my life over again, would I do anything differently? Would I play it safe and never leave Jamaica? Or perhaps I would never have allowed myself to get involved with Christopher's father. If any one of those things were somehow deleted from my life, I would not have experienced Christopher. In fact, the world would not have experienced the Notorious B.I.G. I wouldn't have my grandchildren, and the list goes on.

Life is about living and learning, not regrets. It should be lived to the fullest because this is not a dress rehearsal. I have no regrets—not even being with Christopher's father. I learned some valuable lessons from that experience. I learned well because I didn't repeat my errors. And I wasn't foolish enough to stay with him and, worse, have more kids with him.

It is my hope that young women can be strong enough and firm enough in their morals and beliefs not to be the same fool twice. I don't look down on young girls who court and live with a man and have a baby, then break up with that man and repeat the process, and

life is about living

before they know it, they are twenty-five or twenty-six years old with three babies from three different men. But just know that you, as a woman, are doing a disservice to yourself and your children and are creating a cycle of poverty that is extremely hard to break.

These are the things that need to be taught to the young men and women in the inner city. This is part of my mission, my method of giving back. I believe if you broaden a child's mind through reading and through education, you more than double their chances to succeed in life.

a Life

A life lost
is a life missed;

A life gained
is a life blessed;

A life taken
is a life saddened;

A life given
is a life loved;

A life toiled
is a life honest;

A life lived
is a life remembered.

ACKNOWLEDGMENTS

> I shall
> trust
> and
> be in
> no dread.

I'd like to quote Isaiah 12, verse 2: "Look! God is my salvation. I shall trust and be in no dread. For Jehovah is my strength and my might. And he came to be the salvation of me."

To my mother who instilled in me that honesty is the only way to build my life. My father, who taught me that with love in my heart I will always succeed. My brothers and sisters, for their emotional support. To Faith, I thank you for your constant calls. I know the love is there. God Bless you in all your endeavors. I will be there for you. You will always be my daughter-in-law. Wayne Barrow, I will never regret the day I introduced you as my adopted son. My heart welled just from knowing you and I pray that you are one of the real ones. Mark Piffs, I thank you for being there for my son when he needed you and here for me today. Puffy, we have our silence, heartfelt, rollercoaster moments, there is a lot of love, a ton of confusion, and you still owe me $30,000. No smile, no joke, no flowers. Call me, kid. Sean Carter (Jay-Z) tears are flowing from my eyes just to say thanks. You know "the deal." Thanks, sweetheart, you're one in a million. Buster, thanks for the compliments and the encouragement. Afeni Shakur, thanks friend. The branch has rooted. Artie Erk, thanks for your honesty, straightforwardness, and loyalty. Mrs. Jenny, Beacon Camp is gone but Jenny Cares lives. In such a short time, you have seen me through a lot. I thank you . . . To all my friends at the Effort and Leaders Congregation, thank you for your love, prayers, and insight. Chico, Nino, Clep, Benny Thomas, Dennis, and Goya Horell, thanks. Elisha Silvera, Deborah Nelson, thank you. Your kindness means a lot. Abraham and Wickem, I am glad we know each other. Police Officer Green at the 88th Precinct in Brooklyn, thank you. Drs. Tykott, Mark Grand, Barbara Sehuh, Elisie Alvarez, thank you. Dr. Steven Carroll, thank you for always being there for me when I needed you. Bernard Delano, Kevin, Angel, and Keisha for caring. Donna Vellekemp, Terry Bake, Londell McMillian, Don Cameron, for your wonderful council. Jennifer Smash, you shared a lot. Thanks. Una and Delroy Peterkin, Gloria Landell, the laughter continues. Ed Lover, Dr. Dre, Lisa Evers, Fat Man Scoop, Angie Martinez, thanks for the real love and for making me feel young again. Hazel Thompson, thank you for being my friend. To Tre McKenzie, my coauthor, you were there through the pain and tears, you never gave up on me; through the sleet and snow, you trekked on. You embraced me with kindness and skill. There were times when I wanted to give up but you waited; times when I wanted to scream but you were calm. Thanks for your patience. Ian Kleinert, thanks for the introduction. Sydney, Althea, Bazel, Veron, Charmagne, Balo, Marilyn, Glen, and Paula, thanks for believing in me. Jefferey Tweety, Mary J B., for reminding me that I will always be a mother. To Malaika Adero, my editor, for tactfully informing me not to put off what I can do today, for tomorrow is guaranteed to no one. To my dear friend Zena, "Jehovah is our refuge, his shadow is our shelter, we will not be afraid of anything dreadful by night, nor at the arrow that flies by day," Psalms 91, 1–5.

we will not be
afraid
of anything